Mometrix
TEST PREPARATION

Secrets of the

CPIM®

Strategic Management of Resources Exam Study Guide

DEAR FUTURE EXAM SUCCESS STORY

First of all, **THANK YOU** for purchasing Mometrix study materials!

Second, congratulations! You are one of the few determined test-takers who are committed to doing whatever it takes to excel on your exam. **You have come to the right place.** We developed these study materials with one goal in mind: to deliver you the information you need in a format that's concise and easy to use.

In addition to optimizing your guide for the content of the test, we've outlined our recommended steps for breaking down the preparation process into small, attainable goals so you can make sure you stay on track.

We've also analyzed the entire test-taking process, identifying the most common pitfalls and showing how you can overcome them and be ready for any curveball the test throws you.

Standardized testing is one of the biggest obstacles on your road to success, which only increases the importance of doing well in the high-pressure, high-stakes environment of test day. Your results on this test could have a significant impact on your future, and this guide provides the information and practical advice to help you achieve your full potential on test day.

Your success is our success

We would love to hear from you! If you would like to share the story of your exam success or if you have any questions or comments in regard to our products, please contact us at **800-673-8175** or **support@mometrix.com**.

Thanks again for your business and we wish you continued success!

Sincerely,
The Mometrix Test Preparation Team

Need more help? Check out our flashcards at:
http://MometrixFlashcards.com/CPIM

Written and edited by the Mometrix Exam Secrets Test Prep Team
Printed in the United States of America

TABLE OF CONTENTS

Introduction

Thank you for purchasing this resource! You have made the choice to prepare yourself for a test that could have a huge impact on your future, and this guide is designed to help you be fully ready for test day. Obviously, it's important to have a solid understanding of the test material, but you also need to be prepared for the unique environment and stressors of the test, so that you can perform to the best of your abilities.

For this purpose, the first section that appears in this guide is the **Secret Keys**. We've devoted countless hours to meticulously researching what works and what doesn't, and we've boiled down our findings to the five most impactful steps you can take to improve your performance on the test. We start at the beginning with study planning and move through the preparation process, all the way to the testing strategies that will help you get the most out of what you know when you're finally sitting in front of the test.

We recommend that you start preparing for your test as far in advance as possible. However, if you've bought this guide as a last-minute study resource and only have a few days before your test, we recommend that you skip over the first two Secret Keys since they address a long-term study plan.

If you struggle with **test anxiety**, we strongly encourage you to check out our recommendations for how you can overcome it. Test anxiety is a formidable foe, but it can be beaten, and we want to make sure you have the tools you need to defeat it.

Secret Key #1 – Plan Big, Study Small

There's a lot riding on your performance. If you want to ace this test, you're going to need to keep your skills sharp and the material fresh in your mind. You need a plan that lets you review everything you need to know while still fitting in your schedule. We'll break this strategy down into three categories.

Information Organization

Start with the information you already have: the official test outline. From this, you can make a complete list of all the concepts you need to cover before the test. Organize these concepts into groups that can be studied together, and create a list of any related vocabulary you need to learn so you can brush up on any difficult terms. You'll want to keep this vocabulary list handy once you actually start studying since you may need to add to it along the way.

Time Management

Once you have your set of study concepts, decide how to spread them out over the time you have left before the test. Break your study plan into small, clear goals so you have a manageable task for each day and know exactly what you're doing. Then just focus on one small step at a time. When you manage your time this way, you don't need to spend hours at a time studying. Studying a small block of content for a short period each day helps you retain information better and avoid stressing over how much you have left to do. You can relax knowing that you have a plan to cover everything in time. In order for this strategy to be effective though, you have to start studying early and stick to your schedule. Avoid the exhaustion and futility that comes from last-minute cramming!

Study Environment

The environment you study in has a big impact on your learning. Studying in a coffee shop, while probably more enjoyable, is not likely to be as fruitful as studying in a quiet room. It's important to keep distractions to a minimum. You're only planning to study for a short block of time, so make the most of it. Don't pause to check your phone or get up to find a snack. It's also important to **avoid multitasking**. Research has consistently shown that multitasking will make your studying dramatically less effective. Your study area should also be comfortable and well-lit so you don't have the distraction of straining your eyes or sitting on an uncomfortable chair.

The time of day you study is also important. You want to be rested and alert. Don't wait until just before bedtime. Study when you'll be most likely to comprehend and remember. Even better, if you know what time of day your test will be, set that time aside for study. That way your brain will be used to working on that subject at that specific time and you'll have a better chance of recalling information.

Finally, it can be helpful to team up with others who are studying for the same test. Your actual studying should be done in as isolated an environment as possible, but the work of organizing the information and setting up the study plan can be divided up. In between study sessions, you can discuss with your teammates the concepts that you're all studying and quiz each other on the details. Just be sure that your teammates are as serious about the test as you are. If you find that your study time is being replaced with social time, you might need to find a new team.

Secret Key #2 – Make Your Studying Count

You're devoting a lot of time and effort to preparing for this test, so you want to be absolutely certain it will pay off. This means doing more than just reading the content and hoping you can remember it on test day. It's important to make every minute of study count. There are two main areas you can focus on to make your studying count.

Retention

It doesn't matter how much time you study if you can't remember the material. You need to make sure you are retaining the concepts. To check your retention of the information you're learning, try recalling it at later times with minimal prompting. Try carrying around flashcards and glance at one or two from time to time or ask a friend who's also studying for the test to quiz you.

To enhance your retention, look for ways to put the information into practice so that you can apply it rather than simply recalling it. If you're using the information in practical ways, it will be much easier to remember. Similarly, it helps to solidify a concept in your mind if you're not only reading it to yourself but also explaining it to someone else. Ask a friend to let you teach them about a concept you're a little shaky on (or speak aloud to an imaginary audience if necessary). As you try to summarize, define, give examples, and answer your friend's questions, you'll understand the concepts better and they will stay with you longer. Finally, step back for a big picture view and ask yourself how each piece of information fits with the whole subject. When you link the different concepts together and see them working together as a whole, it's easier to remember the individual components.

Finally, practice showing your work on any multi-step problems, even if you're just studying. Writing out each step you take to solve a problem will help solidify the process in your mind, and you'll be more likely to remember it during the test.

Modality

Modality simply refers to the means or method by which you study. Choosing a study modality that fits your own individual learning style is crucial. No two people learn best in exactly the same way, so it's important to know your strengths and use them to your advantage.

For example, if you learn best by visualization, focus on visualizing a concept in your mind and draw an image or a diagram. Try color-coding your notes, illustrating them, or creating symbols that will trigger your mind to recall a learned concept. If you learn best by hearing or discussing information, find a study partner who learns the same way or read aloud to yourself. Think about how to put the information in your own words. Imagine that you are giving a lecture on the topic and record yourself so you can listen to it later.

For any learning style, flashcards can be helpful. Organize the information so you can take advantage of spare moments to review. Underline key words or phrases. Use different colors for different categories. Mnemonic devices (such as creating a short list in which every item starts with the same letter) can also help with retention. Find what works best for you and use it to store the information in your mind most effectively and easily.

Secret Key #3 – Practice the Right Way

Your success on test day depends not only on how many hours you put into preparing, but also on whether you prepared the right way. It's good to check along the way to see if your studying is paying off. One of the most effective ways to do this is by taking practice tests to evaluate your progress. Practice tests are useful because they show exactly where you need to improve. Every time you take a practice test, pay special attention to these three groups of questions:

- The questions you got wrong
- The questions you had to guess on, even if you guessed right
- The questions you found difficult or slow to work through

This will show you exactly what your weak areas are, and where you need to devote more study time. Ask yourself why each of these questions gave you trouble. Was it because you didn't understand the material? Was it because you didn't remember the vocabulary? Do you need more repetitions on this type of question to build speed and confidence? Dig into those questions and figure out how you can strengthen your weak areas as you go back to review the material.

Additionally, many practice tests have a section explaining the answer choices. It can be tempting to read the explanation and think that you now have a good understanding of the concept. However, an explanation likely only covers part of the question's broader context. Even if the explanation makes perfect sense, **go back and investigate** every concept related to the question until you're positive you have a thorough understanding.

As you go along, keep in mind that the practice test is just that: practice. Memorizing these questions and answers will not be very helpful on the actual test because it is unlikely to have any of the same exact questions. If you only know the right answers to the sample questions, you won't be prepared for the real thing. **Study the concepts** until you understand them fully, and then you'll be able to answer any question that shows up on the test.

It's important to wait on the practice tests until you're ready. If you take a test on your first day of study, you may be overwhelmed by the amount of material covered and how much you need to learn. Work up to it gradually.

On test day, you'll need to be prepared for answering questions, managing your time, and using the test-taking strategies you've learned. It's a lot to balance, like a mental marathon that will have a big impact on your future. Like training for a marathon, you'll need to start slowly and work your way up. When test day arrives, you'll be ready.

Start with the strategies you've read in the first two Secret Keys—plan your course and study in the way that works best for you. If you have time, consider using multiple study resources to get different approaches to the same concepts. It can be helpful to see difficult concepts from more than one angle. Then find a good source for practice tests. Many times, the test website will suggest potential study resources or provide sample tests.

Practice Test Strategy

If you're able to find at least three practice tests, we recommend this strategy:

Untimed and Open-Book Practice

Take the first test with no time constraints and with your notes and study guide handy. Take your time and focus on applying the strategies you've learned.

Timed and Open-Book Practice

Take the second practice test open-book as well, but set a timer and practice pacing yourself to finish in time.

Timed and Closed-Book Practice

Take any other practice tests as if it were test day. Set a timer and put away your study materials. Sit at a table or desk in a quiet room, imagine yourself at the testing center, and answer questions as quickly and accurately as possible.

Keep repeating timed and closed-book tests on a regular basis until you run out of practice tests or it's time for the actual test. Your mind will be ready for the schedule and stress of test day, and you'll be able to focus on recalling the material you've learned.

Secret Key #4 – Pace Yourself

Once you're fully prepared for the material on the test, your biggest challenge on test day will be managing your time. Just knowing that the clock is ticking can make you panic even if you have plenty of time left. Work on pacing yourself so you can build confidence against the time constraints of the exam. Pacing is a difficult skill to master, especially in a high-pressure environment, so **practice is vital**.

Set time expectations for your pace based on how much time is available. For example, if a section has 60 questions and the time limit is 30 minutes, you know you have to average 30 seconds or less per question in order to answer them all. Although 30 seconds is the hard limit, set 25 seconds per question as your goal, so you reserve extra time to spend on harder questions. When you budget extra time for the harder questions, you no longer have any reason to stress when those questions take longer to answer.

Don't let this time expectation distract you from working through the test at a calm, steady pace, but keep it in mind so you don't spend too much time on any one question. Recognize that taking extra time on one question you don't understand may keep you from answering two that you do understand later in the test. If your time limit for a question is up and you're still not sure of the answer, mark it and move on, and come back to it later if the time and the test format allow. If the testing format doesn't allow you to return to earlier questions, just make an educated guess; then put it out of your mind and move on.

On the easier questions, be careful not to rush. It may seem wise to hurry through them so you have more time for the challenging ones, but it's not worth missing one if you know the concept and just didn't take the time to read the question fully. Work efficiently but make sure you understand the question and have looked at all of the answer choices, since more than one may seem right at first.

Even if you're paying attention to the time, you may find yourself a little behind at some point. You should speed up to get back on track, but do so wisely. Don't panic; just take a few seconds less on each question until you're caught up. Don't guess without thinking, but do look through the answer choices and eliminate any you know are wrong. If you can get down to two choices, it is often worthwhile to guess from those. Once you've chosen an answer, move on and don't dwell on any that you skipped or had to hurry through. If a question was taking too long, chances are it was one of the harder ones, so you weren't as likely to get it right anyway.

On the other hand, if you find yourself getting ahead of schedule, it may be beneficial to slow down a little. The more quickly you work, the more likely you are to make a careless mistake that will affect your score. You've budgeted time for each question, so don't be afraid to spend that time. Practice an efficient but careful pace to get the most out of the time you have.

Secret Key #5 – Have a Plan for Guessing

When you're taking the test, you may find yourself stuck on a question. Some of the answer choices seem better than others, but you don't see the one answer choice that is obviously correct. What do you do?

The scenario described above is very common, yet most test takers have not effectively prepared for it. Developing and practicing a plan for guessing may be one of the single most effective uses of your time as you get ready for the exam.

In developing your plan for guessing, there are three questions to address:

- When should you start the guessing process?
- How should you narrow down the choices?
- Which answer should you choose?

When to Start the Guessing Process

Unless your plan for guessing is to select C every time (which, despite its merits, is not what we recommend), you need to leave yourself enough time to apply your answer elimination strategies. Since you have a limited amount of time for each question, that means that if you're going to give yourself the best shot at guessing correctly, you have to decide quickly whether or not you will guess.

Of course, the best-case scenario is that you don't have to guess at all, so first, see if you can answer the question based on your knowledge of the subject and basic reasoning skills. Focus on the key words in the question and try to jog your memory of related topics. Give yourself a chance to bring the knowledge to mind, but once you realize that you don't have (or you can't access) the knowledge you need to answer the question, it's time to start the guessing process.

It's almost always better to start the guessing process too early than too late. It only takes a few seconds to remember something and answer the question from knowledge. Carefully eliminating wrong answer choices takes longer. Plus, going through the process of eliminating answer choices can actually help jog your memory.

Summary: Start the guessing process as soon as you decide that you can't answer the question based on your knowledge.

How to Narrow Down the Choices

The next chapter in this book (**Test-Taking Strategies**) includes a wide range of strategies for how to approach questions and how to look for answer choices to eliminate. You will definitely want to read those carefully, practice them, and figure out which ones work best for you. Here though, we're going to address a mindset rather than a particular strategy.

Your odds of guessing an answer correctly depend on how many options you are choosing from.

Number of options left	5	4	3	2	1
Odds of guessing correctly	20%	25%	33%	50%	100%

You can see from this chart just how valuable it is to be able to eliminate incorrect answers and make an educated guess, but there are two things that many test takers do that cause them to miss out on the benefits of guessing:

- Accidentally eliminating the correct answer
- Selecting an answer based on an impression

We'll look at the first one here, and the second one in the next section.

To avoid accidentally eliminating the correct answer, we recommend a thought exercise called **the $5 challenge**. In this challenge, you only eliminate an answer choice from contention if you are willing to bet $5 on it being wrong. Why $5? Five dollars is a small but not insignificant amount of money. It's an amount you could afford to lose but wouldn't want to throw away. And while losing $5 once might not hurt too much, doing it twenty times will set you back $100. In the same way, each small decision you make—eliminating a choice here, guessing on a question there—won't by itself impact your score very much, but when you put them all together, they can make a big difference. By holding each answer choice elimination decision to a higher standard, you can reduce the risk of accidentally eliminating the correct answer.

The $5 challenge can also be applied in a positive sense: If you are willing to bet $5 that an answer choice *is* correct, go ahead and mark it as correct.

Summary: Only eliminate an answer choice if you are willing to bet $5 that it is wrong.

Which Answer to Choose

You're taking the test. You've run into a hard question and decided you'll have to guess. You've eliminated all the answer choices you're willing to bet $5 on. Now you have to pick an answer. Why do we even need to talk about this? Why can't you just pick whichever one you feel like when the time comes?

The answer to these questions is that if you don't come into the test with a plan, you'll rely on your impression to select an answer choice, and if you do that, you risk falling into a trap. The test writers know that everyone who takes their test will be guessing on some of the questions, so they intentionally write wrong answer choices to seem plausible. You still have to pick an answer though, and if the wrong answer choices are designed to look right, how can you ever be sure that you're not falling for their trap? The best solution we've found to this dilemma is to take the decision out of your hands entirely. Here is the process we recommend:

Once you've eliminated any choices that you are confident (willing to bet $5) are wrong, select the first remaining choice as your answer.

Whether you choose to select the first remaining choice, the second, or the last, the important thing is that you use some preselected standard. Using this approach guarantees that you will not be enticed into selecting an answer choice that looks right, because you are not basing your decision on how the answer choices look.

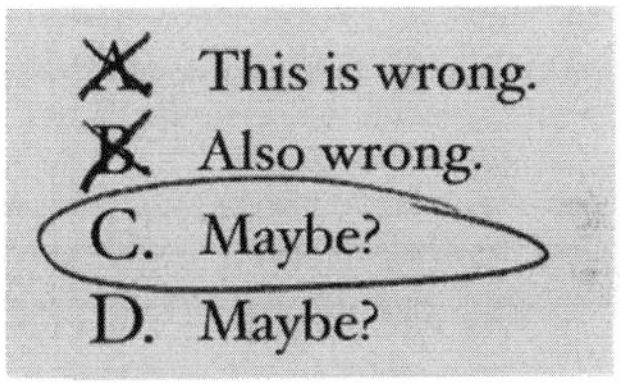

This is not meant to make you question your knowledge. Instead, it is to help you recognize the difference between your knowledge and your impressions. There's a huge difference between thinking an answer is right because of what you know, and thinking an answer is right because it looks or sounds like it should be right.

Summary: To ensure that your selection is appropriately random, make a predetermined selection from among all answer choices you have not eliminated.

Test-Taking Strategies

This section contains a list of test-taking strategies that you may find helpful as you work through the test. By taking what you know and applying logical thought, you can maximize your chances of answering any question correctly!

It is very important to realize that every question is different and every person is different: no single strategy will work on every question, and no single strategy will work for every person. That's why we've included all of them here, so you can try them out and determine which ones work best for different types of questions and which ones work best for you.

Question Strategies

READ CAREFULLY

Read the question and the answer choices carefully. Don't miss the question because you misread the terms. You have plenty of time to read each question thoroughly and make sure you understand what is being asked. Yet a happy medium must be attained, so don't waste too much time. You must read carefully and efficiently.

CONTEXTUAL CLUES

Look for contextual clues. If the question includes a word you are not familiar with, look at the immediate context for some indication of what the word might mean. Contextual clues can often give you all the information you need to decipher the meaning of an unfamiliar word. Even if you can't determine the meaning, you may be able to narrow down the possibilities enough to make a solid guess at the answer to the question.

PREFIXES

If you're having trouble with a word in the question or answer choices, try dissecting it. Take advantage of every clue that the word might include. Prefixes can be a huge help. Usually, they allow you to determine a basic meaning. *Pre-* means before, *post-* means after, *pro-* is positive, *de-* is negative. From prefixes, you can get an idea of the general meaning of the word and try to put it into context.

HEDGE WORDS

Watch out for critical hedge words, such as *likely, may, can, often, almost, mostly, usually, generally, rarely*, and *sometimes*. Question writers insert these hedge phrases to cover every possibility. Often an answer choice will be wrong simply because it leaves no room for exception. Be on guard for answer choices that have definitive words such as *exactly* and *always*.

SWITCHBACK WORDS

Stay alert for *switchbacks*. These are the words and phrases frequently used to alert you to shifts in thought. The most common switchback words are *but, although*, and *however*. Others include *nevertheless, on the other hand, even though, while, in spite of, despite*, and *regardless of*. Switchback words are important to catch because they can change the direction of the question or an answer choice.

✓ FACE VALUE

When in doubt, use common sense. Accept the situation in the problem at face value. Don't read too much into it. These problems will not require you to make wild assumptions. If you have to go beyond creativity and warp time or space in order to have an answer choice fit the question, then you should move on and consider the other answer choices. These are normal problems rooted in reality. The applicable relationship or explanation may not be readily apparent, but it is there for you to figure out. Use your common sense to interpret anything that isn't clear.

Answer Choice Strategies

✓ ANSWER SELECTION

The most thorough way to pick an answer choice is to identify and eliminate wrong answers until only one is left, then confirm it is the correct answer. Sometimes an answer choice may immediately seem right, but be careful. The test writers will usually put more than one reasonable answer choice on each question, so take a second to read all of them and make sure that the other choices are not equally obvious. As long as you have time left, it is better to read every answer choice than to pick the first one that looks right without checking the others.

✓ ANSWER CHOICE FAMILIES

An answer choice family consists of two (in rare cases, three) answer choices that are very similar in construction and cannot all be true at the same time. If you see two answer choices that are direct opposites or parallels, one of them is usually the correct answer. For instance, if one answer choice says that quantity *x* increases and another either says that quantity *x* decreases (opposite) or says that quantity *y* increases (parallel), then those answer choices would fall into the same family. An answer choice that doesn't match the construction of the answer choice family is more likely to be incorrect. Most questions will not have answer choice families, but when they do appear, you should be prepared to recognize them.

✓ ELIMINATE ANSWERS

Eliminate answer choices as soon as you realize they are wrong, but make sure you consider all possibilities. If you are eliminating answer choices and realize that the last one you are left with is also wrong, don't panic. Start over and consider each choice again. There may be something you missed the first time that you will realize on the second pass.

✓ AVOID FACT TRAPS

Don't be distracted by an answer choice that is factually true but doesn't answer the question. You are looking for the choice that answers the question. Stay focused on what the question is asking for so you don't accidentally pick an answer that is true but incorrect. Always go back to the question and make sure the answer choice you've selected actually answers the question and is not merely a true statement.

✓ EXTREME STATEMENTS

In general, you should avoid answers that put forth extreme actions as standard practice or proclaim controversial ideas as established fact. An answer choice that states the "process should be used in certain situations, if..." is much more likely to be correct than one that states the "process should be discontinued completely." The first is a calm rational statement and doesn't even make a definitive, uncompromising stance, using a hedge word *if* to provide wiggle room, whereas the second choice is far more extreme.

☑ BENCHMARK

As you read through the answer choices and you come across one that seems to answer the question well, mentally select that answer choice. This is not your final answer, but it's the one that will help you evaluate the other answer choices. The one that you selected is your benchmark or standard for judging each of the other answer choices. Every other answer choice must be compared to your benchmark. That choice is correct until proven otherwise by another answer choice beating it. If you find a better answer, then that one becomes your new benchmark. Once you've decided that no other choice answers the question as well as your benchmark, you have your final answer.

☑ PREDICT THE ANSWER

Before you even start looking at the answer choices, it is often best to try to predict the answer. When you come up with the answer on your own, it is easier to avoid distractions and traps because you will know exactly what to look for. The right answer choice is unlikely to be word-for-word what you came up with, but it should be a close match. Even if you are confident that you have the right answer, you should still take the time to read each option before moving on.

General Strategies

☑ TOUGH QUESTIONS

If you are stumped on a problem or it appears too hard or too difficult, don't waste time. Move on! Remember though, if you can quickly check for obviously incorrect answer choices, your chances of guessing correctly are greatly improved. Before you completely give up, at least try to knock out a couple of possible answers. Eliminate what you can and then guess at the remaining answer choices before moving on.

☑ CHECK YOUR WORK

Since you will probably not know every term listed and the answer to every question, it is important that you get credit for the ones that you do know. Don't miss any questions through careless mistakes. If at all possible, try to take a second to look back over your answer selection and make sure you've selected the correct answer choice and haven't made a costly careless mistake (such as marking an answer choice that you didn't mean to mark). This quick double check should more than pay for itself in caught mistakes for the time it costs.

☑ PACE YOURSELF

It's easy to be overwhelmed when you're looking at a page full of questions; your mind is confused and full of random thoughts, and the clock is ticking down faster than you would like. Calm down and maintain the pace that you have set for yourself. Especially as you get down to the last few minutes of the test, don't let the small numbers on the clock make you panic. As long as you are on track by monitoring your pace, you are guaranteed to have time for each question.

☑ DON'T RUSH

It is very easy to make errors when you are in a hurry. Maintaining a fast pace in answering questions is pointless if it makes you miss questions that you would have gotten right otherwise. Test writers like to include distracting information and wrong answers that seem right. Taking a little extra time to avoid careless mistakes can make all the difference in your test score. Find a pace that allows you to be confident in the answers that you select.

⊘ KEEP MOVING

Panicking will not help you pass the test, so do your best to stay calm and keep moving. Taking deep breaths and going through the answer elimination steps you practiced can help to break through a stress barrier and keep your pace.

Final Notes

The combination of a solid foundation of content knowledge and the confidence that comes from practicing your plan for applying that knowledge is the key to maximizing your performance on test day. As your foundation of content knowledge is built up and strengthened, you'll find that the strategies included in this chapter become more and more effective in helping you quickly sift through the distractions and traps of the test to isolate the correct answer.

Now that you're preparing to move forward into the test content chapters of this book, be sure to keep your goal in mind. As you read, think about how you will be able to apply this information on the test. If you've already seen sample questions for the test and you have an idea of the question format and style, try to come up with questions of your own that you can answer based on what you're reading. This will give you valuable practice applying your knowledge in the same ways you can expect to on test day.

Good luck and good studying!

Aligning the Resources with the Strategic Plan

Operations Strategy Development Approaches

The four approaches to developing an operations strategy are the overview approach, the trade-off approach, the reductionist approach, and the sequential approach. These different approaches define how management can more narrowly develop a strategy, since there are many considerations. In the overview approach, the method is to consider the primary operational factors such as available resources, technology currently used, capacity for integration, philosophy of quality, and internal company relationships. In the trade-off approach, management considers the interrelationships between operational functions, such as the relationship between customer service and inventory investment or volume of goods produced and cost of goods produced. One function can act as a limit on another. Instead of focusing on and balancing trade-offs, the reductionist approach concentrates on determining the original causes of trade-offs and easing or eliminating them. Finally, in the sequential approach management chooses one of the four competitive priorities (cost, quality, flexibility, or delivery) to focus on, and moves on to another after progress has been made.

Operational Structure

Aligning a company's resources with the strategic plan includes making appropriate operational choices to execute the strategic plan. These operational choices include factors such as the volume and range of products to be produced as well as the operations structure. Structural choices, as opposed to infrastructural choices, are manufacturing decisions that must be made that require large monetary investment and are not easily reversible, such as plant location, plant size, goods produced, manufacturing methods, volume of goods produced, and the extent of staffing. Since these determinations are difficult and costly to change later, they must be thought through meticulously before being made. It is especially important that structural choices reflect the strategic plan.

A company accomplishes its goals according to its operation strategy, planning, and management:

- Operations strategy: Also known as the manufacturing strategy brings together the company vision set forth in the mission statement, corporate strategy, and business strategy with the company's operational reality, or the existing resources and capacity. Through the operations strategy, how to accomplish the goal beginning with the current manufacturing situation is established.
- Operational planning: The development of specific objectives and corresponding performance measures that serve as stepping stones in the process of executing the strategic plan in general and the operations strategy in particular within manufacturing.
- Operations management: The planning and oversight of the manufacturing process, including every step from raw materials to finished goods. Operations management is the day-to-day leadership within manufacturing for executing the operational planning objectives, the operations strategy, and ultimately the strategic plan.

Focused Operations Strategy

One factory cannot effectively accomplish everything. For an operations strategy to be effective in winning market share, it must be focused. There are two main areas operations strategies focus on.

Which focus should be chosen depends on the nature of the business. One focus is process. Process focus is the strategy to be used in environments where many specialized goods are produced in small quantities and may not be repeated, such as in engineer-to-order and make-to-order firms. The manufacturing set-up is generally a job shop. The alternative to process focus is product/service focus. Product/service focus is the strategy to be used in situations where a small number of standard products are repetitively manufactured in large volumes. These goods tend to be produced in dedicated factory lines or cells.

Company Strategy

Without a clear plan for what to accomplish and how to accomplish it, a company will flounder and ultimately lose market share to its competitors. A company strategy is the clear plan for what to do and how to do it that a company needs to stay competitive in the marketplace. In the current global economy, competition is fierce and a company strategy is necessary for success. A good company strategy details the company's goals and how to meet those goals, with due consideration for marketing and operations. The strategy drives the company's resources, or manufacturing operations, in order to meet the goals. If the company strategy and resources/manufacturing operations are not aligned, then the strategy will fail.

Strategic Planning Model

The strategic planning model is a tool for developing a company strategy through framing a mission statement, which serves as the basis for the top-level corporate strategy, including the business strategy, from both of which are created the supporting marketing strategy, financial strategy, engineering or product development strategy, and operations or manufacturing strategy. The strategic planning model is an ongoing process. To remain competitive in the current business environment, a company must be continually evolving to meet rapidly changing demand. Through the strategic planning model, a company can plan and execute appropriate change. An integral part of the process is organizational self-evaluation for strengths and weaknesses.

The following are important terms to understand regarding strategy:

- Mission statement: A succinct presentation of a company's goals and general methods for reaching those goals, as well as the corresponding results to be achieved; a mission statement must be well balanced so that clear direction is given without limiting the company's future scope
- Corporate strategy: An overall plan for the company based on the mission statement, but with specific rather than general goals; the corporate strategy includes the business strategy
- Business strategy: A segment of the top-level corporate strategy in which the direction of the business is set forth; the business strategy should draw from the organization's strengths in order to maximize its competitiveness
- Marketing strategy: A functional plan developed from and supporting the corporate and business strategies defining a company's target market segment, identifying a company's market niche, and evaluating the competition
- Financial strategy: A functional plan developed from and supporting the corporate and business strategies detailing the generation of financial resources (investment strategy) and management of those resources to meet obligations and goals

- Engineering strategy: A functional plan developed from and supporting the corporate and business strategies detailing the framework for designing and developing new products and their corresponding manufacturing processes and supplying the specialized, multi-disciplinary skill sets necessary for both; the engineering strategy can also be called the product development strategy
- Manufacturing strategy: A functional plan developed from and supporting the corporate and business strategies setting forth guidelines for building manufacturing capabilities and infrastructure to fulfill the organizational goals; the manufacturing strategy is often overlooked, and can also be called the operations strategy

Strategic Planning Model Ideal

In the strategic planning model ideal, the mission statement precedes the corporate and business strategies, which precede the functional strategies like the operations strategy. The primary function of the business strategy is to bring the market requirements to bear upon the corporate strategy, but this cannot be done in isolation. Although the operations strategy should theoretically follow the business strategy, knowledge of current operational resources and capability are an essential ingredient in crafting the business strategy in order to avoid unrealistic goals that ultimately cost the company time and money. Determining future direction without first understanding the current reality is a fruitless exercise. There is actually a feedback loop between the two strategies. The operations strategy informs the development of the business strategy, which in turn reshapes the operations strategy.

Strategic Planning Personnel

There are generally three groups of personnel involved in the strategic planning process. These three groups are outside or external stakeholders, top-level company management, and general management and special staff. The outside or external stakeholders are individuals or groups outside of the company who have a vested interest in the company's success, including the company's suppliers, customers, and stockholders, related unions, and the community at large. Top-level company management is comprised of the company's senior management team. General management and special staff include lower-level management such as departmental leaders and personnel with special expertise necessary in the planning process.

Business Strategy Development Methods

The three methods generally used for developing business strategies are:

- Price leadership: The business strategy is based on low product prices. A range of products are manufactured through a reliable and respected process and sold for comparatively low prices.
- Product differentiation: The business strategy is based on unique product characteristics that set the product(s) apart from the competing product(s).
- Customer focus: The business strategy is based on meeting customer needs and providing a high level of customer service and responsiveness.

Business Process Reengineering

Business process reengineering or redesign (BPR) is the thorough analysis and complete overhaul of a company's current mode of operating, emphasizing processes and process customers. Tools utilized to perform BPR include participative or concurrent engineering, understanding and documenting the current business process in-depth, and clearly defining the business needs and strategic goals. All processes are then realigned to actually meet the stated needs and goals, especially as related to cost, quality, and speed. No method is retained that is not economic and effective. The goal is radical improvement without regard to how things have been done in the past.

The current operating parameters within a system are often considered requirements even though they may not be. Circumstances may have changed without a corresponding requirements update, or the operating parameters may never have been required to begin with. External critical input is a worthwhile asset in evaluating the current operating parameters and establishing up-to-date requirements to be met through business process reengineering (BPR). Determining the actual requirements and preparing the requirements document is the responsibility of the project team and the key system users. The requirements themselves, any potential problems, existing skill sets, training needs, transaction volumes and timing, and management approval must all be considered.

Manufacturing Strategy Development

There are many considerations involved in developing a manufacturing strategy. The manufacturing strategy is often overlooked, but can provide long-term competitive edge if handled well. Some of the manufacturing strategy considerations include the facilities, especially their location and price; capacity, especially technology and price; quality, both goals and inspections methods; information systems, and how they relate to competition; organization of staff, centralized or decentralized; integration, determining what functions to perform internally and what to delegate to suppliers; and processes and technologies, especially preventive maintenance to avoid breakdown and stoppage costs.

Aligning Resources

The purpose of aligning resources with the strategic plan is to increase a company's competitiveness within the marketplace. A company can align its resources with the strategic plan and thus increase its market share by creating and maintaining a strategic environment, by structuring operations to execute the company strategy, and by developing infrastructure to execute the company strategy. A strategic environment can be fostered by creating a company strategy using the strategic planning model. Structuring operations and developing infrastructure to execute the strategic plan involve making structural and infrastructural decisions that support the company strategy.

Order Qualifiers

Order qualifiers are company or product characteristics that must be in place for customers to consider purchasing the goods in question; a common example of an order qualifier is price: potential customers have budgetary restrictions, so products outside of their price range are not considered, but products within their price range must meet other criteria to be purchased. Order qualifiers are the company or product characteristics that cause potential customers to consider buying a product, but many companies may produce products with the appropriate order qualifiers for a given customer. Products with the required order qualifiers are acceptable to the customer, but that does not mean that the customer will buy them.

Order Winners

Order winners are usually one or perhaps two company or product characteristics upon which customers base their decision to buy the product in question; an order winner is the standout company or product quality that causes the customer to choose a company's product over viable competitors; order-winning strategies include price, quality, delivery speed, delivery reliability, customer service level, flexibility, product design, and image; to be effective, companies must focus on only one or two order winners. An order winner is the distinctive competency that causes the customer to choose one product in particular over the other acceptable alternatives. An order winner is the characteristic that sets the product apart from other products with order qualifying characteristics. Some examples:

- Price: The price is the amount of money a business charges its customers for the product. Price is made up of cost, which is the amount of money the business spends manufacturing the product, and profit. A business can reduce its price by reducing costs, often through reducing time. Price is typically an order qualifier rather than an order winner. Customers will not buy items that are too expensive, but they will not choose the least expensive, either, if it means accepting low quality, unreliable delivery, or other order disqualifiers. Industry market leaders often charge the most, not the least, for their products.
- Quality: Like price, quality is often an order qualifier rather than an order winner. Customers cannot always differentiate the quality levels of their competing suppliers, unless, of course, the quality is poor. An important distinction to make in considering product quality is the difference between actual quality and perceived quality. Customers may perceive products with packaging that looks cheap or other superficial tags as being poor quality, even though they meet all stated specifications. Actual and perceived quality must be at an acceptable level for consideration of the product in the marketplace, even more so than price.
- Delivery speed: The length of time it takes for a company to get their product to the customer from the time that the customer orders it. Delivery speed can serve as an order winner because shorter lead times attract customers hoping to reduce their own inventory. Shorter lead times also make forecasting easier. Quick delivery speed is beneficial to the supplier as well, since it decreases the length of time between taking orders and receiving payment for those orders. Increasing delivery speed can be complex in the current manufacturing environment where inventory is usually minimized. Delivery speed can be increased through distribution networks that keep products close to customers, but with the disadvantage of inventory costs. Another option is overnight delivery. Since predictable demand is essential to maintaining delivery speed, one solution is to give the customer the impression of a short lead time by establishing long-term contracts that are called off as needed by the supplier and delivered quickly after call-off.
- Delivery reliability: A company's ability to deliver a product at the time agreed upon. Delivery reliability is crucial to manufacturers, since they often use the product soon after receipt. Late deliveries can slow down or even halt manufacturing, so on-time delivery is certainly an order qualifier, and can even be an order winner. Suppliers often do not measure or poorly measure their delivery reliability, so customers may need to monitor it themselves.
- Customer service: Includes all aspects of interfacing with buyers, from delivery speed and reliability to positive staff attitudes when interacting with customers to responsiveness to customer emergencies. All of these facets combine to form a powerful order winner. To make sure that customers are receiving the full benefit of their supplier's customer service, the supplier may need to educate them about the customer service level achieved. For example, a customer may not realize or appreciate consistently reliable delivery if they use a safety lead time to protect against late deliveries.

- Flexibility: The manufacturer's ability to adapt and adjust to change and unexpected events. This makes it possible to produce exactly what the customer wants, including customization and optional features, when the customer wants it, as well as to introduce new products and forego imposing large lot quantities on customers. Different aspects of manufacturing flexibility are total volume flexibility, product mix flexibility, labor flexibility, and new product flexibility. Flexibility enables a company to keep up with current market trends and customer needs. Flexibility is an order winner in situations when the market demand and/or customer needs are rapidly changing.
- Product design: The process of developing a new product. The process begins with customer needs. Through the product design process, these needs are defined as product specifications that drive the design process. The effectiveness and speed with which a company learns, quantifies, designs for, and meets customer needs in the marketplace is crucial. It is an order winner. If product design is slow, the product may be obsolete before it is available. Meeting customer needs and desires before the competition does provides competitive edge and market share.
- Image: The perception of the company or product in the marketplace. In some industries, image is of paramount importance. Two examples are the make-up and food industries. When a company focuses on its corporate and product image as its order winner, large sums must be spent on advertising to create and maintain the image.

Competition and Company Strategy

Within the marketplace, companies compete for market share. A company competes for market share in the marketplace by developing and executing a company strategy. Executing the strategy is the transformation process. A company rises above the competition by having a better company strategy than their competitors have and/or by executing their strategy better than their competitors do. When this is the case, a company gains the highest portion of market share and becomes the market leader. It is the possession and execution of a good company strategy that makes a company competitive in the marketplace.

Customer Service

Customer service is generally the ability of a company to respond effectively and quickly to customer requests; specifically, a general, organizational performance measurement in which the percentage of customer orders delivered on time is tracked.

Customer service level is the general, organization-wide customer service performance measurement comprised of the percentage of customer orders delivered on time. In make-to-stock production environments, the customer service level is the percentage of customer orders, order line items, or order dollar values filled from stock upon receipt. In design-to-order and make-to-order production environments the customer service level is the percentage of orders delivered by the agreed-upon date; customer service level is measured with regard to a predetermined target level. Customer service level is also called the customer service ratio.

Customer Relationship Management

Customer relationship management (CRM) is a business and marketing strategy in which the customer is the central consideration. CRM is accomplished through improvement in every aspect of customer service, including fast and effective order entry, on time and accurate delivery, and responsiveness to customer needs and requests. CRM includes obtaining feedback from customers to further improve service. The ultimate goal of CRM is the development of lifetime customers through building long-term relationships that are beneficial to both manufacturers and their customers. Lifetime customers are important because maintenance of current customers is less expensive than finding new ones, long-term customer relationships result in manufacturers' better understanding and meeting customer needs, and repeat business and referrals from current customers due to faithful service.

Identifying Customer Wants

The identification of customer wants begins with identification of the customer: the next manufacturing work center, the end user of the product, or anyone in between. After identifying the customer, the method of collecting information from the customer must be determined and utilized. Customer wants data can be gathered through customer or market surveys, product complaints, or in-depth research including personal interviews by market research firms. The third and final step in identifying customer wants is analyzing and summarizing the information collected for use in design and development.

The analysis of customer wants is used as the basis for product planning and design and process planning and design. In product planning, the information is used to develop appropriate technical specifications, which are converted into component characteristics in product design. Manufacturing methods capable of fabricating the specified product are selected, and process control methods to certify the desired quality level are implemented.

Quality Function Deployment

Quality function deployment (QFD) involves a seven-step plan diagramed as the house of quality to effectively and efficiently utilize customer wants data in the design and development process. Step 1 is a statement of the customer attributes. These are the attributes the customers desire in the product. Step 2 is the sequence of importance, a prioritization of the customer attributes according to customer preferences. Step 3 is customer perception, the customers' view of how the company and/or product compares to competitors for each customer attribute. Step 4 is product characteristics, how each customer attribute could be met or fulfilled in the product. Step 5 is the product characteristics and customer attributes matrix, which weighs the relationship between customer attributes and product characteristics. Step 6 is the relationship characteristics, the interrelationships between product characteristics whether beneficial or adverse. Step 7 is technical points, the technical specifications, technical difficulty, target measurements, costs, and more for each product characteristic.

Fulfilling Company Strategy

Role of Quality

Quality systems and tools such as building quality into the design, quality at the source, continuous improvement, process improvement, mistake proofing, fail-safe work methods, and quality circles reduce costs, improve products and company effectiveness, and decrease overall lead times. In short, to improve quality is to increase competitiveness, and to increase competitiveness is to better fulfill the strategic plan. Although the specific quality systems and tools utilized will vary greatly among industries and companies, quality is always an important tool in achieving strategic goals since it increases competitiveness. Each company must develop its own quality program based on its own environment and goals.

Role of Information Systems in Aligning the Resources

Information systems are an important aspect of a company's infrastructure that can enhance or detract from competitiveness. Information systems are utilized at every level and in every department, and must be appropriate for these individual and group uses as well as support the company-wide strategic plan. Information system choices include system architecture and networking, supplier and customer interfaces, knowledge-based systems, decision support systems, data capture and bar coding. The current trend in information systems is toward decentralization. Workers and departments have their own individual computers and systems, which are integrated into the company network, instead of one mainframe controlled by one specialized department.

Manufacturing Environments

The four types of manufacturing environments are:

- Job shop (high variety, low volume): A manufacturing facility in which a wide range of general equipment is organized according to function and staffed by skilled personnel who can follow specifications for specialized products. Goods go through production according to a specified routing, which is different for each item produced. Goods are produced according to the individual customer's requirements, and small numbers of a wide variety of items are manufactured. Quality and timeliness are key.
- Batch manufacture (somewhat high variety, somewhat low volume): Similar to job shop, but on a larger scale with less specialization, so there is somewhat less variety and greater volume produced. Batches of goods are produced to fill a wide range of orders, but orders are repetitive, or even standard. Since there is repetition, standing routings and manufacturing instructions as well as tooling and fixtures are provided. Capacity requirements planning (CRP) is employed.
- Line manufacture (somewhat low variety, somewhat high volume): Line manufacturing is a manufacturing environment in which specialized equipment is used to produce a limited range of similar, standardized goods in somewhat high volumes. All of the goods produced proceed through the same line, or sequence of manufacturing operations. Mixed-model and rate-based scheduling, master production scheduling (MPS), and material requirements planning (MRP) are used.
- Continuous manufacture (low variety, high volume): Continuous manufacturing is similar to line manufacturing, but with even more specialized equipment and less variety of goods produced. It is a manufacturing environment in which highly specialized equipment is used to produce one or a very few type(s) of set goods in high volumes at an extremely low cost. Product changes and new products occur rarely. Manufacturing occurs twenty-four hours per day and seven days per week.

Variety and Volume

The variety and volume of goods produced determine the manufacturing environment needed. A company should first determine the volume and variety of products necessary to reach their strategic goals, and then establish a manufacturing environment accordingly. Volume refers to the number of items produced, while variety refers to the number of types of items produced. There is an inverse relationship between the two. Factories usually make large amounts of a few set products, or small amounts of many specialized products.

Financial Considerations

High-volume and low-variety manufacturing are usually paired. High-volume, low-variety manufacturing is generally the least expensive production method for a given product, and is thus employed when a company has chosen price as their order-winning strategy. These factories typically produce only one product, or a handful of similar products.

Low-volume and high-variety manufacturing are also usually paired. Low-volume, high- variety manufacturing is typically employed when a company has chosen customization or quality as their order-winning strategy. Within this manufacturing environment, inventory investment and other associated costs are high because of the large number of raw materials and components required.

Part commonality, the purposeful use of parts already stocked when designing new products or processes, is a strategy for minimizing these costs.

Product Life Cycle

A product's position in its life cycle significantly affects the type of manufacturing environment necessary to meet the demand for the product. In general, low manufacturing volume is sufficient in the early stages of the life cycle, followed by increased volume as the market responds to the new product, and ending with low volume as the product's life closes. The six life-cycle stages are pre-product development, product development, testing and introduction, rapid growth, steady state, and phasing out. It may be necessary to have different manufacturing methods at different stages. Demand forecasting must be used for each stage. Even after the product's life cycle ends support and spare parts must be available for those still in use in the field.

The six phases of the product life cycle:

- Pre-product development: General research, not geared toward a particular product but that informs the decision-making process for what product(s) to pursue.
- Product development: The process of designing a particular product that has been earmarked through pre-product development and market research.
- Testing and introduction: The process of establishing product specifications and forecasting and filling early demand for the product.
- Rapid growth: The stage at which the product has been fully launched and demand for it rises.
- Steady state: The stage at which the product is firmly established in the market and seasonal and other demand trends can be predicted and filled.
- Phasing out: The end of the product life cycle, marked by decreasing demand, either by the company's choice to introduce a new replacement product or by external market forces.

Production, Layout, and Cellular Manufacturing

Project production is a production process in which major, specialized products, such as capital equipment or structures, are ordered and completely designed and produced in response to the order, often in the quantity of one

Traditional layout is a factory organizational scheme, in which similar machines are grouped together into work centers, and batches are transported between work centers as specified in their product routings; the traditional layout tends toward longer queues and lead times; the traditional layout is also called the functional layout

Cellular manufacturing is a factory organizational scheme in which equipment is grouped together to make a particular part; parts move one by one between the machines in the cell; because the cellular layout tends toward shorter move times, queues, and lead times, smaller space requirements, and simpler scheduling it is recommended for just-in-time (JIT) manufacturing

Group Technology and Synchronized Production

Group technology is a factory organizational scheme in which product design and process attributes are analyzed and products are grouped for production in work cells according to similarity in order to standardize processes and set-ups times so goods progress through the factory at a faster rate

Synchronized production is a factory organizational scheme in which all activities at all levels are governed by the overall manufacturing goals; at every level of manufacturing, goods are produced in the quantity and at the time necessary for the next manufacturing level to meet the overall manufacturing goals, so work in progress and semi-finished goods are minimized and not held in storage

In-House Development Versus Software

The primary consideration in implementing change in information systems is that the new system needs to meet the requirements. Since all businesses are different, there is no single best option when it comes to software. Software can be developed internally, or a wide variety of software packages can be purchased. Not only should the new system theoretically meet the predefined requirements, but there should also be system testing and simulation to verify that the system actually meets the requirements and to smooth out glitches. Choosing a software package entails submitting requirements to possible suppliers, reviewing the supplier proposals, arranging demonstrations and supplier discussions for the better options, discussing options with system users, and making a selection. Implementing the new system requires general and specific training for the users as well as deciding how the system will be used in the business environment. The software itself should not be revised, but rather additional modules and transactions should be added on as necessary. This makes system updates and technical support simpler.

Replacing Management and Systems

Some of the benefits and financial savings to be expected when a company replaces or modifies its existing production and inventory management system include reduced inventory and a resulting reduction in inventory cost; enhanced customer service, through more accurate timing and a higher rate of on-time deliveries; increased productivity, through better utilization of facilities and more effective scheduling and management of inventory; lower material costs; lessened incidence of expediting and obsolescence; higher accuracy of costing, financial, and decision-making information; greater responsiveness to market changes; and, through any or all of these benefits, improved competitiveness in the marketplace. The nature and extent of the benefits reaped depend on the company's former position, the position to which it is moving, and the process chosen to make the changes.

The Potential Costs to Be Incurred When Replacing or Improving a Company's Production Management and Inventory Control System

Typical costs incurred in replacing or improving a company's production management and inventory control system include the purchase price of necessary hardware and software, both of which can be capital investments; the cost of additional work on the system such as interfaces and add-ons; the internal labor rate for conversion of data from its existing format to the format required by the new system; the expense of reorganizing inventory storage and operations to flow with the new system; the cost of education and training for all affected personal, which is estimated by some sources to be as high as the cost for the system itself; consulting fees for external critical input; and salary for a dedicated project manager. The range and level of costs incurred are variable and situational. The investment is usually recouped in about one year following implementation.

Functional and Process Layouts

Functional or traditional manufacturing layouts are centered on the machinery and equipment and include job shops and batch manufacturing. Similar processes or skills are grouped together into work centers, and products move from work center to work center to receive the necessary processing. This has been used in the past with low-volume manufacturing, but that practice is changing somewhat in the current manufacturing environment. Process layout is centered on the product itself. The process is developed and equipment placed as necessary for production of a particular item or family of items, as in line and continuous manufacturing, work cells, and group technology layouts. Process layouts are used for high volume manufacturing.

Determining Factory Location

The proximity to both suppliers and customers is an important consideration in determining factory location. Proximity to suppliers is important because of the cost of transporting the raw materials or other components to the factory, especially if the goods are expensive or difficult to transport. Proximity to suppliers is also important because the knowledge base of the materials supplied tends to be greater in the area where the goods are produced and supported. Proximity to customers is important to decrease delivery lead-time and maximize responsiveness. Ideally, a plant should be located close to its suppliers and customers, but in the real world both are rarely possible. Sometimes one is not even possible. Locating the plant near a transportation center or employing a distribution network can be stopgap strategies when proximity is not possible.

Important Considerations

Distribution methods: Distribution method refers to how a factory gets its products to its customers. Distribution method is an especially important consideration when a factory is not located close to its customers, or when the factory produces goods for a geographically broad range of clients. Storing products near major markets for increased customer responsiveness can be a good idea. Alternatively, if the factory is located near a major transportation center, items can be stored at the factory, and shipped nationally and even internationally as needed. The rate of demand and cost of transport and storage are factors that determine is the more viable option: distribution networking or central storage and transport.

The availability of utilities and labor: Utilities are necessary for manufacturing and thus must be available, but this is not always the case at locations remote from industrial centers. Road, telephone, power, water, and other systems must be in place and capable of handling the level of demand placed on them by a manufacturing facility. Availability of labor refers to more than people to work in the plant. People with the required skill sets and experience must be available to work in the plant. Relocating people and installing utilities are possible to meet these needs, but the associated costs may be prohibitive.

Tax rates, labor wages, and building and operation costs: These costs vary with location, and tend to decrease as distance from an industrial center increases. Additionally, governments in high-unemployment or underdeveloped areas may provide incentives such as tax and/or transport concessions to encourage the establishment of business. The cost of land, construction materials, the actual construction, and utilities are all included in building and operation costs. Decreasing these costs can give a competitive advantage if they do actually result in overall decreased costs for the company, but other costs such as transportation and relocation of skilled personnel may increase due to location.

Facility Design Decisions

Decisions related to facility design must be made very carefully since they affect the company's future and are difficult and costly to change later. Understanding the past decisions resulting in the current facility design is an important step in the decision-making process. Facility design decisions include location, size, and integration level of the facility. The determination of the facility location hinges on several factors, such as proximity to suppliers and customers, distribution method and access to transportation, availability of utilities and labor with the necessary skills, and local taxes, wages, and building and operation costs. The choice of facility size is dependent on the facility focus as set forth in strategic planning. Bigger is not necessarily better. Already existing large facilities can be segmented into several smaller sections, each with a clear focus. Integration level decisions include the extent of vertical, backward, and forward integration.

Structural Decisions

Because the operations strategy includes structuring manufacturing and facilities to execute the strategic plan, structural decisions are part of developing an operations strategy. The four primary areas to structure are:

- Organizational design involves the type of production process (project, job shop, batch, line or continuous) and the production layout (traditional, cellular, group technology, synchronized, or a combined or specialized layout).
- Capacity increases can be based on leading demand, lagging demand, or tracking/chasing demand strategies, and can also be accomplished through higher work force levels, overtime, and subcontracting.
- Facility decisions include location, size, and integration level.
- Technology decisions are based on the manufacturing focus, either process or product, and involve how to execute production.

Integration

Important Types of Integration

- Integration: The extent to which a manufacturing organization internally completes operations necessary for fabricating their product(s)
- Vertical integration: The extent to which a manufacturing organization internally completes operations necessary for fabricating their product(s) from the initial raw materials to the final sale to the consumer
- Backward integration: The process of looking back from a company's current manufacturing scope, up the supply chain, and assimilating those previously supplied functions internally into the company
- Forward integration: The process of looking ahead from a company's current manufacturing scope toward distribution and sales to the end user and assimilating those previously supplied functions internally into the company

Ramifications of Backward and Forward Integration

When a company chooses backward integration, they are replacing goods they previously purchased with internally supplied goods. Assuming that the company can do as good a job as their former supplier at the decreased production volume, they decrease costs by cutting the supplier's profit margin. Additionally, information sharing can be more open than is the case when the supplier also sells goods to competitors.

In implementing forward integration, a company is entering into distribution and retail sales, both of which vary greatly from manufacturing. Advantages include cutting out middleman profit margins and receiving more direct feedback from end users.

There are advantages in both cases, but these advantages hinge on the company's success in accomplishing a challenging task, which is not guaranteed.

Factory Focus

The concept of factory focus entails narrowing the scope of operations in order to concentrate on areas of expertise and the business focus. In operating a focused factory, an organization depends on external suppliers operating in their areas of expertise and business focus rather than utilizing lesser products or services internally manufactured or performed. Integration is the opposite of focus. It is a broadening of operations to include functions previously performed externally to cut costs and simplify relationships. The current trend in manufacturing is for companies in highly specialized fields to focus on single level fabrication, while companies involved in simpler processes implement vertical integration.

Technology Decisions

Choices regarding the technologies utilized are part of developing and implementing an operations strategy. The technologies involved are the support systems for operations. These decisions should be based on the manufacturing focus, and ultimately the operations strategy. In manufacturing with a process focus, there is a wide range of goods being produced through the same processes. A system for interfacing with the supplying manufacturing groups is required. In manufacturing with a product focus, a few items are produced through a broad range of processes. The stand-alone nature of product-focused manufacturing lends itself to simpler support systems. Factory location is another factor in technology choices, especially in relation to material replenishment systems. Suppliers close by can restock through a kanban system, while long lead times and safety stock are realities for planning materials from distant suppliers. Similarly, support for more sophisticated technology is not easily accessible from remote locations and is a consideration.

Operations Infrastructure

Operations infrastructure includes services and frameworks that enable the operations structure to function. The infrastructure includes the participation of employees in the life of the company, the organizational design of employee and management relationships, and the quality and information systems in place. Infrastructure differs from structure in that it is easier to change, but it still plays a significant role in accomplishing the strategic plan. Infrastructure is important because of the contribution it makes to company productivity, and ultimately company competitiveness. Infrastructural choices must be made with the company strategy and manufacturing processes in mind since the infrastructure must support both the strategy and the processes in place.

Relationship Between Infrastructure Choices and Productivity

A company's productivity is its ability to produce goods and/or services, or its production effectiveness. For a company to survive and excel in the competitive market it must continually improve its productivity. The best method for increasing productivity is focusing on people. Since operations infrastructure includes the people issues of employee involvement and employee relationship to management (organizational design), it is clear that the people are a major part of the infrastructure. Operations structure, especially the personnel aspects, is crucial to company productivity, and increasing that productivity hinges on good infrastructural choices over time.

Cross-Functional Problem Solving

A cross-functional problem solving team should include the marketing and sales, engineering and design, manufacturing, quality assurance, costing, and materials departments. Involving multiple disciplines simultaneously in the problem solving process optimizes time and cost required to solve problems. The marketing and sales department contributes their expertise in customer needs and desires; engineering and design contribute technical and design skills for understanding what went wrong and redesigning accordingly; manufacturing contributes expertise in how to produce parts, and certifies that any new or redesigned parts are not problematic from a production standpoint; quality assurance verifies adherence to quality standards in processes and products, as well as troubleshooting poor quality as a potential source of the problem; the costing department assesses the financial impact of potential problem resolutions for feasibility; and the materials department handles issues of material availability, timing of material changes, and obsolescence.

Employee/Workforce Involvement

The purpose of employee involvement is to utilize the ideas of all employees at all levels within the company, to develop the employees, to create feelings of ownership and pride among the employees toward the company and their job function, and to free managers to orchestrate overall progress rather than the day-to-day operations. Employee involvement produces responsibility at the source, which is the concept of workers taking full ownership for performance and improvement of their own functions. The most important factor in developing healthy employee involvement in a company is the attitude of management. Management must believe that workers at all levels can solve problems, and enable them to do so. Management can foster workforce involvement by developing an infrastructure that provides education and incentive. Some specific tools used to encourage employee involvement are suggestion programs, quality circles, cross-functional problem solving teams, appraisal and reward systems, and education and training.

The following employee involvement tools:

- Suggestion programs: Formal methods of encouraging employees to develop and submit ideas for improving the business; all employees are eligible, and "winning" or "accepted" suggestions are typically implemented and rewarded in some way
- Quality circles: Small groups of employees who work together as a team, and additionally spend time (typically one hour per week) meeting together with the purpose of improving their product and/or process
- Cross-functional problem solving teams: Teams of employees from different departments within the company who combine their expertise to solve a particular problem
- Appraisal and reward systems: Methods of encouraging employee participation and excellence in achieving company goals by evaluating employee work and compensating and recognizing employees for progress made and/or objectives accomplished
- Education and training: Instruction for employees at all levels in job-specific skills, cross-functional skills, and basic skills to enable them to better contribute to the company

Suggestion Programs Versus Quality Circles

Suggestion programs and quality circles are similar in that both are methods through which employee participation in company improvement is encouraged. They are different in how the participation is encouraged. Suggestion programs are competitive, oriented toward independent individual participation, and often overlook suggestions for small improvements. Quality circles focus on cooperative participation and teamwork, and it is usually small improvements that are implemented. The accumulated small improvements add up to large savings and quality improvement. The goal of both suggestion programs and quality circles is to utilize the full potential of all workers, but quality circles are much more successful in this aim.

Fostering Successful Quality Circles

There are many important factors in running successful quality circles. They can be summarized into three categories: the leadership, the workers, and the structure of the quality group itself. Leadership entails all levels of leaders, from the direct supervisor of the quality group all the way up to top-level management. Leadership support of the groups is essential, as is the skill of the group supervisor in focusing on the goal and facilitating the meetings. The workers themselves must feel ownership of their process or product and be willing to identify and solve problems. Some essential characteristics of the quality groups is that they remain small, focus on work-related problems, receive proper training in problem solving and working as a group, and meet consistently and frequently.

Organizational Structure

Terms of Structure

- Organizational structure: The company hierarchy; the interrelationships between different departments as well as between managers and employees
- Organization structure chart: A diagram detailing the organizational structure; also called an "org chart"
- Simple structure: An organizational structure in which the top company leader oversees the team of leaders that run the company's departments; simple structures are typically utilized in small companies
- Divisional structure: An organizational structure in which the company is divided into stand-alone segments that function separately
- Group structure: An organizational structure in which multiple legally separate companies operate under and support a parent company

Review Video: Corporate Organizational Structure
Visit mometrix.com/academy and enter code: 752986

Effect of Organizational Focus

The presence or absence of manufacturing focus, as well as the nature of that focus, exert a profound influence on a company's organizational structure. Organizational design is the concept of structuring the interrelationships of leadership, staff, departments and responsibilities within a company to facilitate meeting the strategic plan. Manufacturing focus can be either product- or process-oriented. Product-focused manufacturing tends toward decentralization, marketing, and market responsiveness. Process-focused manufacturing tends toward centralization and slow response to market change, but with the advantage of specialized staff. Both company size and policy also play an important role in organizational structure.

Downsizing/Right Sizing

A recent trend in manufacturing has been organizational streamlining, downsizing or right sizing. This trend involves the removal of unnecessary tasks and functions from a business, to allow the business to focus on its primary goal without the distraction of nonessential services and functions that can be contracted or outsourced when needed. Another method of streamlining is breaking down a single complex organization into multiple smaller businesses each with a single focus. Either way, this downsizing reduces waste, expenses, layers of management, and staffing needs, producing a leaner and more effective business environment with simpler organizational structures.

Centralization/Decentralization and Levels of Management

A centralized organizational structure is one in which control and decision-making reside with upper management and not within the operations areas themselves. Conversely, a decentralized organizational structure is one in which control and decision-making do not reside with overall management but rather within the operations areas. An example is a company with several manufacturing sites. One office can run all of the sites, or each site can run itself within the company policies.

Levels of management refer to the layers of people between the actual operations and the top leader. Simpler organizational structures have fewer levels of management, increasing flexibility and decreasing non-value-added activities and time required for making decisions.

Multi-Disciplined Teams and Company Communications

In the past, organizational structures have been organized according to isolated departments, but have recently shifted toward joint endeavors. Instead of working on projects serially (one department followed by another), they are being handled in parallel (multiple departments involved simultaneously), decreasing the time to market, lead times, and costs. Working together is more efficient than working alone. Even upper level management is following this trend.

Company communication, most importantly that between managers and workers, can be formal or informal, one-way or two-way, managerial or relational. The trend in today's manufacturing environment is informal, two-way, and relational, also known as "management by walking around." Memos from the office do not build company commitment like face-to-face interaction does.

Organizational Change in Marketplace

Globalization has increased business competition, and the trend will only continue. To continue to compete in the global marketplace, businesses must change. They must continually improve or they will not succeed. Large organizations are breaking themselves down into smaller business units or companies to focus on one product or expertise. Conversely, smaller organizations are joining together to increase business volume and/or geographical reach. Keeping pace in the current marketplace requires keeping pace with new technologies and business management concepts, such as business units, reduction in levels of management, supply chain management, etc. A business that waits too long to implement improvements will fail.

Supply Chain

Terms of Supply

- Supply chain: The overall material flow in providing products and services, including the string of processes and companies from raw materials to end products used by consumers; the components of the supply chain are supplier, producer, distributor, retailer, and customer
- Supply chain management: The holistic orchestration of internal and external material flow through the supply chain
- Supplier: A component of the supply chain that sells or provides goods and/or services; an organization from whom a company buys goods and/or services
- Producer: A manufacturer; this component of the supply chain is associated with the value chain
- Distributor: An individual or organizational component of the supply chain that serves as a middleman by purchasing and reselling goods
- Retailer: An individual or organizational component of the supply chain that purchases goods from a producer or distributor and resells them to consumers
- Customer: An individual or organizational supply chain component that receives a product or service from an organization and is external to that organization, but not necessarily the ultimate consumer
- Value chain: The operations within a company through which the products and/or services pass and receive value before being sold to customers

Supply Chain Management

The focus of supply chain management is material flow. Materials management, materials departments, and logistics are all, to a certain extent, precursors to supply chain management. Materials, and thus supply chain management, are crucial in manufacturing because materials are typically the largest cost incurred by manufacturers. The central role of materials in manufacturing, the material costs incurred, and the resulting profitability or lack thereof make effective supply chain management prerequisite to financial success. Good supply chain management encompasses better and more economical material flow, both internally and externally. Linking the end demand back through all stages of the chain eliminates expensive and unnecessary inventory at intermediate stages.

Stages of the Value Chain

The stages of the value chain are demand, material supply, manufacturing, finished goods storage, and distribution. A company's value chain begins with established demand. Demand is established through demand forecasting or orders received, depending on how the company operates. From there, material must be planned and acquired for manufacturing to meet the demand. Following material planning and acquisition is the actual manufacturing of goods. Once the goods are manufactured, they are stored in finished goods inventory. From finished goods inventory, goods are distributed from the factory to the customer. Distribution centers and inventories located near customers may be part of the distribution process.

Concepts Upon Which Effective Supply Chain Management Rests

Effective supply chain management rests upon specialization, information sharing, communication, management support, inventory reduction, and cooperation. An entire supply chain is made up of many companies working together. Specialization is important because each company in the chain has its own job to do, a job at which that company excels, increasing overall effectiveness. Information sharing across the supply chain is essential so that each company is working with all pertinent information to do the best job overall. Similarly, clear and open communication between the companies is needed for effectiveness. Support of top management is necessary, as well as inventory reduction, if the supply chain is to be managed for the good of all. Unwillingness to relinquish large inventories cancels out the financial benefits of supply chain management. In summary, effective supply chain management rests on cooperation. All of the companies in the chain work together in cooperation, rather than in competition. Mutual trust, communication, information sharing, inventory reduction, and specialization are all part of the cooperation necessary to achieve success.

Role of Technology

Information technology has progressed rapidly in recent history. Not that long ago faxes replaced telex machines. Since then, cell phones, laptops, networking, and the internet have been introduced. All of these technologies enable instantaneous data communication, heightening companies' abilities to function as effective links in the supply chain. In fact, the widespread availability of these technologies and the resulting instantaneous data communication has made them necessary for companies to remain competitive in the marketplace. This field as a whole is referred to as e-commerce. Effective e-commerce results in rapid information flow, better planning, and reduced costs, all of which help companies meet their strategic goals and increase their competitiveness and profit margin. Current e-commerce technologies in use include automated warehouses, computer aided design, computer aided engineering, data warehouse, decision support systems, electronic data interchange, electronic funds transfer, electronic mail, internet, intranet, online procurement, and point of sale data capture.

Information Technologies Used in the Supply Chain

- Automated warehouses: Inventory storage facilities employing computer control and high-rise palletized racking systems in which an operator commands the system to store incoming goods and retrieve outgoing goods; inventory location and quantity information is held in the system compute
- Computer aided design (CAD): A design process in which the designer(s) use(s) specialized software instead of draft boards enabling increased storage and easier analysis, development, and breakdown of designs
- Computer aided engineering: An engineering process in which specifications are generated and tested using specialized software instead of manual calculations
- Data warehouse: Computerized data storage for data used in conjunction with decision-making software applications
- Decision support systems (DSS's): Specialized software used by managers to quantitatively evaluate potential scenarios and relevant factors in the decision making process
- Electronic data interchange (EDI): The paperless transfer of information between company computer systems, using a standardized data format
- Electronic funds transfer (EFT): The paperless transfer of money between companies and/or banks using computer systems
- Electronic mail (e-mail): Paperless, internet-based messaging system between individuals and/or companies via computers
- Internet: Worldwide information exchange powered by a global computer network formed through connecting individual computers and computer systems with telecommunications hardware
- Intranet: A localized internet, usually within one company
- On-line procurement: Direct, electronic ordering and purchasing of goods and services through the internet or by accessing a supplier's computer system
- Point of sale data capture: The process of recording sales information when retail sales are made to produce customer bills and sales analysis and replenishment planning data

Information Technology Application

Supplying Manufacturing Companies

In the past, supplying manufacturers was a simple process. The manufacturer submitted an invoice to the supplier. The supplier responded with delivery of the requested goods and an invoice. The manufacturer then paid the invoice. Over time, this process has changed. Long-term relationships exist between suppliers and manufacturers. Instead of single orders and corresponding invoices, deliveries are made according to a schedule and tallied in weekly or monthly invoices. They can be tallied as quantities of items or standard containers delivered. Another innovation is not tallying the deliveries at all, but back flushing through the number of items produced by the manufacturer to determine the number of supplied parts used and paying accordingly. All of these transactions between suppliers and manufacturers rely on the data transfer methods in use.

Supplying Retailers

In the past, supplying retailers was a simple process. The retailer submitted a purchase order to the supplier. The supplier responded with delivery of the requested goods and an invoice. The retailer then paid the invoice. Over time, this process has changed. Long-term relationships exist between suppliers and retailers. Merchandisers employed by the supplier actually place the products on the retail shelf, increasing the number of deliveries and eliminating the need for retail inventory. A step beyond merchandising is vendor-managed inventories. Through point of sale data capture, the supplier knows when to replenish the stock on the retailer's shelves and does so, and the retailer does not even keep records of deliveries made. Alternatively, large retailers may maintain central warehousing and distribution where deliveries are made, and suppliers are paid for goods delivered. All of these transactions between suppliers and retailers rely on the data transfer methods in use.

International Issues

Primary Obstacles to Be Considered Before Sourcing or Outsourcing Globally

The primary difficulties encountered in global sourcing and outsourcing are transportation, communication, payment, and governmental regulations. Transportation is an issue due to the distance and expense involved in international shipping. Communication is even more complex. International business communication is hindered by time, language, and cultural differences. Payment for goods is not straightforward because of differing currency and currency fluctuations. Governmental regulations differ from country to country, and can impact the method of payment, required documentation, currency exchange control, and more. Some countries also require counter or reciprocal trading and/or investment in their country.

Rationale for and Means of Establishing International Outsourcing

International outsourcing can be established directly by researching, contacting and buying from international companies, or indirectly through using an agent, representative, or distributor located within the buyer's country. Using a local representative is a good way to buy internationally without facing the associated problems. The middleman handles the problems, and is compensated accordingly. Companies buy internationally despite the obstacles for many reasons. Like products may not be available locally; international prices may be lower; quality, delivery speed, and/or delivery reliability may be better. Companies gain international business by establishing and excelling in their order winning strategy.

Terms of Sourcing and Distribution

In sourcing: Internally supplying goods and/or services instead of relying on external suppliers; in sourcing can be chosen for many reasons, including capacity available for use or unreliable external supply.

International distribution: The process of delivering goods and/or services to customers in other nations; the four primary international distribution channel strategies are exporting, licensing, joint ventures, and direct ownership.

Exporting: An international distribution channel strategy in which a company continues producing in their current mode and ships the goods abroad to international customers, either because the company was approached by a foreign customer, the company actively sought foreign customers, or the company sells to a middleman in the foreign country.

Licensing: An international distribution channel strategy in which a home company certifies a local company in another country to manufacture their product under their name with their expertise, support, and advice in return for payment; licensing saves the home company the cost of international shipping and operations while still making some profit off international markets.

Joint ventures: An international distribution channel strategy in which a home company joins forces with a local company in another country to produce the home company's product there; the home company invests capital and management; joint ventures give the home company the advantage of using an existing manufacturing and distribution system instead of building one.

Direct ownership: An international distribution channel strategy in which the home company develops a completely new manufacturing and distribution system in another country; the home company assumes maximum risk and cost in comparison to other international distribution channel strategies, but also maximizes their profits and control

Distribution channels: The means of transporting goods from manufacturing to the final consumer; in international distribution the three primary distribution channels are direct shipments, consolidation shipments, and local distribution

Direct shipments: A distribution channel in which goods are packaged at the manufacturer and delivered from there to the customer

Consolidation shipments – A distribution channel in which goods from multiple companies are combined and shipped together when each company's volume was not high enough to justify direct shipment; goods are sent to a central location to be packed together, then shipped, and finally unpacked and distributed appropriately after reaching their destination

Local distribution: A distribution channel in which a company has enough customers in another country to open a distribution center there, where bulk direct shipments are received and then redistributed to local customers

International Distribution

Transportation Methods

Intermodel transportation is used for international distribution. Intermodel transportation is defined as the use of two or more modes of transportation to deliver goods from the manufacturing site to the end customer. Typically, surface transport such as road or rail is used to transport material from the manufacturing site to an airport for air transport or a port for sea transport. Movement by air is preferable for low-weight, high-value goods because of the high cost, and movement by sea is preferable for high-weight, low-value goods. Then the goods are surface transported to their final destination. If there is a land connection between the point of origin and the final destination, surface transport can be used exclusively.

Trading Groups

Three trading groups have emerged on the international scene: North America, Europe, and the Pacific Rim. The North American group was formed by the North American Free Trade Agreement (NAFTA) and consists of Canada, the United States, and Mexico. The European Union is the world's largest individual market, and contains most European nations. The Pacific Rim is formally named the Asia-Pacific Economic Cooperation and includes most nations with coastline on the Pacific Ocean. The European and North American blocks are considered the most powerful, but the Pacific Rim block is expected to surpass the European market as the largest market in the near future. Competing effectively in the international market requires third-party verification(s) such certification and world-class status.

FLEXIBILITY

It is important for a company, products, and personnel to exhibit a variety of flexibility:

- Total volume flexibility: A company's ability to adapt and change the overall number of goods produced while maintaining competitiveness and financial integrity. Achieving total volume flexibility requires a low break-even point. The break-even point is the lowest percentage of manufacturing capacity at which the company does not lose money. Total volume flexibility can be developed by basing manufacturing operations on small, simple, inexpensive, multi-purpose equipment operated by cross-trained personnel rather than large, expensive, dedicated equipment. This allows incremental changes in production output.
- Product mix flexibility: A company's ability to vary the parts or products being produced while maintaining competitiveness and financial integrity. It allows production of a wide variety of goods to meet demand. Achieving product mix flexibility requires short set-up times for operations. Mixed model scheduling is also a helpful tool in achieving product mix flexibility.
- Labor flexibility: The ability of a company's personnel to perform different jobs as necessary to meet customer demand. It allows personnel to be moved around as needed to meet goals, which is especially important in overload situations. Labor flexibility requires cross training and rotation of personnel as well as willing attitudes on the part of personnel. It can be considered the counterpart of specialization.
- New product flexibility: A company's ability to bring new products to market with minimal disruption. This is especially important in industries and markets where change is frequent and inevitable. New product flexibility can be developed by expanding and maintaining alternatives in product families where change is expected and not making decisions too early.

CHAIN OF TRANSFORMATIONS

The chain of transformations, or the transformation process, is the sequence of steps from initial inputs to final outputs, from raw materials to finished goods. The sequence is divided into five specific steps:

- Primary resource creation: The initial attainment of raw materials, such as mining ore. Primary resource creation companies are considered non-manufacturing producers.
- Fabrication of parts: Production of goods that are not finished products themselves but rather are used to build other products.
- Assembly: The process of constructing a finished product from parts. Both parts building and assembly companies are considered manufacturers.
- Distribution: The process of transporting finished goods, and can be performed internally by the producer/manufacturer or externally by a distribution company.
- Service and delivery: Entails customer interactions such as sales and product delivery transactions. Distribution and sales and delivery companies are considered service companies.

DEMAND

In the leading demand method, the decision to increase manufacturing capacity is based on demand forecasting. Leading demand is used when a company has enough confidence in their forecast of increased sales to increase their capacity in anticipation, to avoid insufficient capacity in the future. The disadvantage is the cost of underutilized capacity if the predicted sales do not materialize.

In the lagging demand method, the decision to increase manufacturing capacity is based on actual demand. Lagging demand is used when a company is uncertain of future sales, so capacity increase is postponed until actual demand is established. The disadvantage is that the capacity may limit sales before it is updated if there is increased demand.

In the tracking/chasing demand method, the decision to increase manufacturing capacity is based on actual demand and incremental demand increases. Tracking demand is a compromise between the leading and lagging demand methods. Like lagging demand, the disadvantage is the amount of time necessary for capacity increases, although incremental increase can be implemented more quickly.

Time-Based Competition

Time-based competition (TBC) is a corporate competitive strategy focused on eliminating time waste in manufacturing. TBC is implemented by reducing the lead times and lead time variations that affect customers through analyzing and improving the design, manufacturing, and transportation processes. More specifically, TBC is implemented and lead time and lead time variation are reduced through setup time reduction, elimination of non-value adding activities, stabilization of cycle time, and process improvement. Effective TBC results in improved customer responsiveness, and good customer responsiveness, especially in comparison to the industry market, increase competitive advantage.

Reducing Lead Time

Lead time is typically reduced by reducing setup time, lowering batch size, and eliminating unnecessary queuing. Setup time reduction is important because it enables batch size reduction. The most economical and time-effective batch size is one, but batches must be larger than one to offset the cost of setup. When setup is reduced, the batch size can come closer to one. Queue time is a major component of lead time, and can be minimized through installation of work cells or manufacturing lines or increase of available capacity. Work centers and manufacturing lines operate on a product-based flow, so goods are fed from operation to operation without waiting, decreasing inventory and work in process as well. Increasing the capacity allows handling of greater work volume, so fewer goods have to wait for processing.

Reducing Setup Time

It is important to reduce setup time because setup consumes capacity without any corresponding production. Furthermore, since setup consumes available capacity, it decreases the productive capacity. Time spent setting up is time not spent manufacturing. Another reason to reduce setup is that setup time determines the batch size. Ideally, the batch size should be one, but the setup time requires a minimum batch size to justify the setup cost. Decreasing the setup time decreases the minimum batch size, and decreasing the batch size decreases the work in process and overall lead time. Setup times should be continually monitored to identify long and problem-causing setups as well as the progress made in reducing them. Setup time reductions of 75 to 90% are feasible through simply rethinking the setup process, eliminating unnecessary aspects, and better organizing the worker's essential tasks. One related concept is single minute exchange of dies (SMED). Goals for set-up time reduction should be 50% decrease, followed by another 50% decrease, ultimately ending in single digit minutes.

Cycle Time

Cycle time is the length of time necessary to manufacture one production unit, the length of time between the completion of one production unit and the next, or the length of time from a material's entrance into until its exit from a manufacturing plant. Cycle time is usually calculated as the inverse of the production rate, or the length of time necessary to manufacture one production unit. Unstable or irregular cycle times disrupt smooth operational flow and cause erratic demand for materials and production. Stable cycle times allow pacing of manufacturing and material demands. Long cycle times lead to high work in process inventory. Short, stable cycle times are preferable to minimize lead time and increase time-based competitiveness.

Relationship Between Customer Responsiveness and Time-Based Competition

Increasing time-based competitiveness, which is achieved through reducing lead time, shortens the time necessary to provide products to customers and respond to customer requests for product and/or delivery changes. Faster delivery and response times mean increased flexibility, customer responsiveness, and customer service level. In short, effective time-based competition (TBC) improves customer responsiveness. Eliminating time waste, the premise of time-based competition (TBC), decreases a company's costs and increases their competitiveness while also improving their flexibility. Monitoring internal, industry-wide, and industry leader customer service levels helps a company position itself competitively in the marketplace to meet customer needs.

Lead Time Reducing, Waste Eliminating, Process and Product Improving Manufacturing Strategies

- Lean production: A manufacturing strategy utilizing multi-skilled workers and highly flexible machines in which input resources are minimized to reduce costs by waste elimination and process simplification; in lean production a broad product range is manufactured
- Total quality management (TQM): A manufacturing strategy requiring the participation of all workers at every level to improve processes, products, services, and even the manufacturing environment to achieve customer satisfaction and competitive success
- Just-in-time manufacturing (JIT): A manufacturing strategy comprised of waste elimination, continuous process and product improvement, minimization of inventory, and lead time reduction
- Agile manufacturing: A manufacturing strategy focusing on cost, quality, dependability, and flexibility to manufacture and sell a wide product range
- Theory of Constraints (TOC): A manufacturing strategy based on logistics, performance measurements, and thinking process tools; TOC logistics management includes drum-buffer-rope scheduling, buffer management, and VAT analysis; in TOC, throughput, inventory, and operating expense performance are measured and the five focusing steps are performed; TOC thinking process tools include identification of problems through the current reality tree, identification and development of solutions through the evaporating cloud and future reality tree, and implementation of solutions through the prerequisite and transition trees

Mistake-Proofing and Fail-Safe Methods

Mistake proofing is the practice of developing processes, particularly set-up and manufacturing operations, in such a way that errors leading to product defects are identified and corrected. The goal of mistake proofing is to reduce the number of incorrectly assembled parts, and to keep defective parts from continuing in the manufacturing flow. One example of mistake proofing is counting the components used in assembly and not letting a manufacturing batch proceed if an incorrect number of components have been used.

Fail-safe work methods involve designing operations such that incorrect actions cannot be completed. The goal of fail-safe work methods is to reduce the number of mistakes made in manufacturing. Examples of fail-safe work methods include computer systems that require verification when entries are outside of the expected range or tooling that does not release manufactured goods until the correct processing has occurred.

Decentralized Computer Systems

The use of integrated but decentralized computer systems provides many advantages, since it maintains the primary advantage of centralization while minimizing the disadvantages. The effects of system failures are contained locally, rather than felt universally as they would be in a centralized system; data input is controlled by the actual users and operators rather than by unrelated specialists, resulting in decreased or even nonexistent lead times for data entry; costs for information systems are decreased since the function is integrated into normal operations rather than maintained as a separate, specialized department; and the information sharing of centralization is still available through the use of local area networks (LAN's).

Information Systems

Role of Information Systems in Supplier and Customer Interfacing

In the current manufacturing environment of long-term supplier partnerships, rapid and accurate transfer of information between suppliers and their customers is an important consideration. It is not uncommon for the supplier to have access to limited portions of their customer's information system to facilitate the transfer of customer requirements and changes. The primary advantages of these arrangements are the time saved and the quality of data transmission. Installing a customer "work station" at the supplier that is linked to the customer's network, electronic data interchange (EDI) by linking the customer and supplier's systems together, and the internet are all tools for establishing such a supplier interface.

Similar to supplier interfacing, customer interfaces are also an important competitive tool in the marketplace. The speed, efficiency, and effectiveness with which companies receive and respond to customer orders are crucial. The technologies and methods that can be employed for customer interfacing are the same as those for supplier interfacing.

Role of Software Packages in Manufacturing Information Systems

There are many software packages currently on the market for manufacturers to use in or as their information systems. Manufacturing resource planning (MRPII) is a far-reaching system integrating all aspects of running a manufacturing business. The goal of the software is to increase the company's competitiveness .The software can be grouped into two types, knowledge-based and decision support systems. Knowledge-based systems make decisions internally based on input data, data relationships, and set logic and trigger the necessary actions to keep manufacturing on schedule. Material requirements planning (MRP) rescheduling logic is an example of a knowledge-based system. Decision support systems do not make decisions, but rather aid managers in decision making through analysis of potential outcomes. An example of a decision support system is rough-cut capacity planning.

Data Capture

Capturing data is of central importance since data is the basis of future planning. As technology and the manufacturing environment have changed, so has the mode of capturing data. Currently, bar coding, scanning, and programmable logic controllers (PLC's) are widely used tools to capture data. Bar coding is the use of a series of thick bars, thin bars and spaces to represent numbers and letters. The code is "read" using electronic wands and scanners. Like the information systems themselves, data capture has become decentralized. Data is typically recorded as it is generated in the place it is generated, rather than relegated to a centralized system with the ensuing delays.

Bar Coding

On the manufacturing floor, bar codes are often used for keeping track of work in progress (WIP), and later for finished goods held in storage. Manufacturers also label goods with bar codes at the insistence of their customers, the retailers. One code is used for the individual items, and a different corresponding code is used for cases of items. Retailers use the bar coding at the point of sale to record information, maintain current stock records, access up-to-date pricing, and generally reduce mistakes. The bar codes themselves are simple and becoming increasingly common.

User Documentation and Pilots

User documentation refers to the information resources available to system users and system user trainees. User documentation can exist in the form of manuals or job-specific training notes and transaction instruction sheets. The user manuals can easily become impractical to use, while the training notes and instruction sheets are practical and relevant since each worker uses only the ones that apply.

A conference room pilot is an offline simulation of the new system used for testing, experimentation, and simulation training. It is a middle ground used to verify theoretical decisions and train operators before implementation on the factory floor.

Aspects of Engineering

Engineering is the overarching process of designing a product and designing and implementing economic production means for that product. The engineering function can be broken down into three aspects: design engineering, industrial or manufacturing engineering, and maintenance engineering. Design engineering is the actual design of the product, including verification of its quality, manufacturability, and economic feasibility. Industrial or manufacturing engineering is the development of an economically feasible production process for the designed product, including determination of manufacturing layout and methods used. Maintenance engineering is the preventative and corrective upkeep of manufacturing equipment. Design engineering and maintenance engineering are particularly important in just-in-time (JIT) manufacturing since the industrial engineers specify the manufacturing layout and methods and the maintenance engineers keep the equipment functioning.

Methods of Financial Settlement

Financial settlement methods are the means by which suppliers receive payment from their customers for goods and/or services. The method of financial settlement utilized hinges upon the quality of relationship and the ordering process employed between the supplier and customer. Traditional one-time purchase orders are paid after the goods are received and verified. Other methods such as ongoing purchase orders and scheduled releases are verified as they are delivered and paid per time period. Suppliers who have demonstrated their reliability may be paid without verification. Certified suppliers delivering to the point of use are not verified, but are paid per time period by back flushing through goods produced by the manufacturer to determine the number of supplier's items consumed.

Statistical Process Control

Statistical process control (SPC) is a process quality measurement system in which a process is maintained within an acceptable operating range through measurement, feedback, and correction of process variables. SPC results are reported in graphical form so that any changes or problems in stability or tolerances are quickly and easily observable. Process measurements are plotted on the vertical axis, along with applicable engineering tolerances and control limits, against time on the horizontal axis. Engineering tolerances are based on specified requirements, while control limits are set according to actual process performance. As sources of process variation are identified and removed, the control limits can be tightened. The control limits must be equal to or within, preferably within, the engineering tolerances for the process to be under control.

Statistical Process Control Terms

- X charts: A statistical process control (SPC) chart in which average process measurements are graphed against time to indicate process trends, whether deterioration, improvement, or steadiness.
- R charts: An SPC chart in which process measurement ranges are graphed against time to indicate process stability or the lack thereof (erraticism).
- P charts: An SPC chart in which the percentage of a process attribute that is found to be nonconforming is recorded against time.
- C charts: An SPC chart in which the observed number of a process attribute that is found to be nonconforming is recorded against time.

Financial Performance Measurements

The following financial performance measurements:

- Inventory investment: The amount of money a company spends on inventory, including the cost of raw materials and components, work in process, and finished goods and their associated inventory holding costs; inventory investment is combined with the cost of manufacturing and compared to proceeds from sales to determine profitability; ideally, the inventory should be limited to the number of goods needed to operate manufacturing and provide customer service
- Inventory turnover is a measurement of the effectiveness of inventory management based on the length of time a company holds its inventory calculated by dividing the annual cost of sales by the value of the average inventory held or the value of the inventory held at the end of a given period; higher inventory turns indicate better production and inventory management
- Return on investment (ROI): Financial performance measurement of yield or payback on an expenditure calculated by subtracting associated costs from generated income and dividing the difference by the investment made; ROI is increased by reducing cost and/or investment
- Product cost measurements: Financial performance measurements for gauging direct and indirect costs to a company for generating a product, including material, labor, and overhead costs
- Direct labor cost measurements: Financial performance/product cost measurements of the portion of product cost due to labor actually performed in manufacturing the product, traditionally through efficiency and utilization, but more currently through performance to plan; the cost of labor, time variances, and labor flexibility are also direct labor cost measurements
- Indirect labor cost measurements: Financial performance/product cost measurements of the portion of product cost due to general labor performed in the company that allows the product to be manufactured, particularly supervision and management; a supervisor's staff's performance, ability to motivate workers and build a team atmosphere, and future planning are all indirect labor measurements.

- Materials cost measurements: Financial performance and product cost measurements of expenditures made for materials used in manufacturing; materials cost measurements include the cost of purchased materials, the cost of materials processing, the processing yield of materials, material usage variances, inventory holding costs, and inventory level monitoring with respect to a specified target.
- Overhead cost measurements: Financial performance and product cost measurements of expenditures made for manufacturing that are not easily attributable to particular products or processes and usually divided into departmental, factory, and general categories; the idea of distributing overhead costs indiscriminately among products has somewhat fallen into disrepute of late, leading to the rise of methods such as activity-based costing

Roles of Direct and Indirect Costs and Direct and Indirect Labor

Direct product costs are those costs that are incurred through the actual production of the product, like the purchase price of raw materials and operation of processing machinery used. Indirect product costs are general and facility costs incurred that allow manufacturing of the product but are not attributable to particular products or processes, like utilities for the facility. Similarly, direct labor costs are incurred through the labor performed to build the product or perform the service in question. Indirect labor costs are incurred through general work that allows production to happen but is not specific to any one product or process, like supervision, management, and janitorial services. Direct labor costs have dropped due to automation.

Problems That Arise in Indirect Labor That Should Be Reflected in Indirect Labor Performance Measurements

A lot of indirect labor is invested in manufacturing products, and each type has its own weaknesses. Manufacturing supervision easily gets bogged down in day-to-day tasks such as inspection and rework at the cost of future planning. Engineering and design staff tend toward long delays in and poor communication of product development. The tendency of finance and accounting personnel is to make precise measurements too late to do any good. Customer service departments can get caught up in the details of order processing and become a significant but unwarranted portion of the product lead time. In any department or expertise lack of workforce flexibility is problematic. All of these negative tendencies must be monitored and curbed.

P:D Ratio

P:D ratio is the ratio of the overall manufacturing lead time to the delivery time required by or promised to the customer; as the customer's desired delivery time decreases, so must the manufacturing lead time decrease to maintain flexibility; if the manufacturer's lead time does not correlate well to the delivery time, then inventory is used to meet demand, and higher inventory means decreased flexibility

Cycle Time Performance Measurements

Lead time costs money. Longer lead times lead to higher levels of work in process (WIP), lower levels of flexibility, and longer range future forecasting and the resulting decrease in forecast accuracy. These are the reasons just-in-time (JIT) manufacturing focuses on lead time reduction. Lead time is affected by every step of the manufacturing process. Measuring these specific times that contribute to the overall lead times for correlation to the standard times set as well as for improvement purposes serves as a useful organizational metric. Specific times measured can include development of products, selection of suppliers, preparation of the master schedule and budget, receipt of ordered materials, return of customer calls, entry of sales orders, changeover of machines, the wait between packaging and shipping of finished goods, the update of inventory files, and various meetings. Any of these activities can progress slowly and absorb unnecessary time, resulting in unnecessary expense.

Supplier Response Measurements

The length of time spent in receiving goods from suppliers is one component of product lead time. In the current market, where supplier partnerships are the norm, the customer and supplier work together to expedite the delivery process. Customers provide suppliers with information regarding forecast demand, so the supplier can better prepare for future customer demand. Some specific metrics gauging supplier response time include the percentage of orders delivered on time, the percentage of items or shipments found to be below the acceptable quality level (AQL), the number of demand or requirement changes successfully handled by the supplier per period, and supplier lead times for items needed sporadically rather than regularly.

Speed and Time Measurements

It is common for standard times to be set only for direct-labor manufacturing tasks, limiting the usefulness of time metrics. Alternatively, standard times can be determined for indirect-labor tasks, or productivity can be measured through counting activities performed per time period rather than timing them individually. Some time performance measurements like these include the average time required for product testing, the number of deliveries made by a vehicle per time period, the length of time required to order goods, and the time required by inventory personnel to provide the materials to manufacturing for a work order. These types of tasks can be monitored and improved departmentally.

Configuring and Integrating the Operating Processes to Support the Strategic Plan

Business Sales Categories

Companies typically fall into one of two categories when it comes to sales. The first category of companies is those that make the products they want to make, and then try to sell those products in the marketplace. The other category is those companies that cater to the marketplace by making the product(s) demanded, and going further than that by making the demanded product(s) better than their competitors do. The companies that produce goods to meet demand are said to be *marketplace-driven.* The demand in the marketplace is determined through market research, which includes market analysis, sales analysis, and consumer research and can be conducted by the company itself, its designee, or independent parties.

Manufacturing Planning and Control System

A manufacturing planning and control system consists of three levels: the first level of top management planning, the second level of operations management planning, and the bottom level of operations management execution. Top management planning encompasses business planning and sales and operations planning. It feeds into operations management planning. Operations management planning, including master production scheduling and materials requirements planning, feeds into operations management execution. Operations management execution encompasses procurement, kanban control, and production activity control. Additional elements of manufacturing planning and control are resource requirements planning, associated with sales and operations planning; rough-cut capacity planning, associated with master production scheduling; capacity requirements planning, associated with material requirements planning; and distribution planning and planning data within operations management planning.

Elements of a Manufacturing Planning and Control System

- Business planning: The top management planning function in which an overall future plan for the organization is created, including organizational direction and anticipated business volume
- Sales and operations planning: The top management planning function of developing an overall production plan based on the business plan, manufacturing resources and financial resources; the approved production plan is a commitment to manufacturing and an authorization to proceed
- Resource requirements planning: A tool used in top management planning to verify the feasibility of the production plan developed in sales and operations planning by comparing it to the available resources
- Master production scheduling: The operations management planning function of developing a detailed production plan, also known as an anticipated build schedule, from the more general production plan; the master production schedule (MPS) serves as the basis for all other manufacturing plans and schedules
- Rough-cut capacity planning: A tool used in operations management planning to verify the feasibility of the MPS by comparing it to the available manufacturing capacity
- Distribution planning: The operations management planning function of managing the dispersion of finished goods through controlling finished goods inventory supply and replenishment

- Material requirements planning (MRP): The operations management planning function of determining a detailed material plan derived from the detailed material requirements, for both purchasing and internal manufacturing, to meet the MPS
- Capacity requirements planning (CRP): A tool used in operations management planning to break down the material plan into the individual operations required and compare them to the availability of the work centers involved
- Planning data: All of the information that is used to support operations management planning including item master files, bills of material, and routing files
- Procurement: The operations management execution function of acquiring the materials necessary for production in a timely manner
- Production activity control (PAC): The operations management execution function of controlling the volume of material in production through input-output control and establishing manufacturing priorities through dispatching
- Kanban control: The operations management execution function of replacing manufacturing materials as they are used; kanban control can be used in tandem with or in place of PAC

Operations Management

Interaction with Other Departments

All aspects of a manufacturing business interact with each other and depend on each other for success. The operations management system in is no different. The marketing and sales function provides the demand forecast which drives operations, including product requirements, market trends, market prices, volume, and competitor status. The engineering and design function handles product design and modifications, as well as plans financially feasible production methods for the products that are ultimately carried out by operations. The logistics function handles all materials, including acquiring, storing, and distributing operations inputs and outputs. The finance and accounting function administers the company's finances, and can pinpoint existing and potential financial problems in operations. The human resources function manages personnel issues such as recruiting, education and training, employee development and evaluations, and other personnel policies, which provide and enable operations workers to perform their jobs. Each department must be set up to fulfill the company's objectives, and they must furthermore interact with each other in a way to fulfill those objectives.

Operations Management System Configuration with Regard to Top Management Planning

Top management planning includes business planning and sales and operations planning. The business plan is a company's long-term future plan, usually for five years or more, and part of the planning process is verifying the availability of facilities and resources to support the plan. The business plan informs the sales plan and production plan, which are the blueprints for executing the long-range business plan in the near and intermediate future, based on sales forecasts and manufacturing and financial resources. The sales plan specifies what products will be sold by period, and the production plan specifies what products will be produced by period. The production environment is set by considering the range and volume of items to be produced, either job shop, batch manufacturing, line manufacturing, or continuous manufacturing. Top management planning, through the business plan, sales plan, and production plan, provides the input that drives operations. The operations management system must be configured to support the execution of top management planning.

Operations Management System Configuration with Regard to Operations Management Planning

The operations management planning function consists primarily in establishing the master production schedule (MPS) and deriving the material requirements plan from the MPS. Operations management develops top-level management's production plan into an MPS, or anticipated build schedule. The MPS states finished goods to be produced per day or week, a much finer time period than the production plan details. The feasibility of the MPS is verified through rough-cut capacity planning. Material requirements planning (MRP) is performed to supply materials as needed for production to execute the MPS. Through MRP, net material requirements are calculated while maintaining manufacturing priorities to determine what supplies to order, when to order them, how much to order, and when to have them delivered. This is called the material plan, and its feasibility is verified through capacity requirements planning (CRP).

Cost Management

The area of cost management is comprised of cost composition, the relationships between cost and process and technology decisions, and associated methods of cost accounting, asset valuation, and financial settlement and their application. Cost management systems serve three purposes: inventory valuation for accounting purposes, operations cost control through providing costing information to production management, and product costing to determine the company's actual expense incurred for products. Historically, the largest cost in production was labor, but recently both material and overhead costs have grown beyond labor costs, and costing systems must be adjusted accordingly.

Terms of Cost Management

- Product cost: The actual expense incurred by a company in manufacturing a product, comprised of the costs of labor, material, and overhead; the product cost is determined through allocation methods
- Cost composition: The breakdown of the elements adding up to the product cost: labor, material, and overhead
- Labor cost: The expense incurred paying the workers who manufacture a product; labor cost is calculated by multiplying the standard hours required to produce an item by the labor rate
- Material cost: The direct cost of the materials used in producing an item, including the purchase price as well as subsequent internal costs like goods receiving and storage
- Overhead cost: The indirect costs of manufacturing like equipment depreciation and management salaries; overhead costs can be specific to a work center through which an item was processed or more general, applying to the whole facility; overhead costs are determined by estimating indirect costs, allocating non-productive costs, and calculating and allocating the overhead costs

Project Planning

Projects must be thoughtfully planned out so that there is a blueprint or map for achieving project goals, and a specific means of progress accountability. The length of time for project completion should be limited to avoid confusion and ambiguity, as can occur if the project lingers through a management change. The best timing for implementation is during a slow month, so glitches can be worked out and workers can adjust without the excessive pressure to perform that would be present at a critical time. The project plan should exist in two forms, an outline with the major milestones, their due dates, and actual completion dates as they occur for management and a detailed work plan including specific tasks and responsibility assignments for personnel. Project plans are typically maintained on project planning software for ease in tracking, updating, making changes and generating reports.

Implementation Phases

Determining phases of implementation entails deciding how much of a project to implement at a time. This issue is simplified when the project scope is limited to one factory, or when computerizing an environment with little or no previous computerization. One implementation method is the module-by-module approach, where one module of the project is implemented at a time until all have been completed. This decreases confusion, and allows more resources to be focused on the module being implemented. Phased implementation is more difficult when the project scope encompasses multiple factories or replacing multiple independent computers or computer systems with an integrated package. In this case, large portions or the whole project is usually implemented at one time, following extensive testing and test transfers to assure the success of the change.

Statement of Work and Responsibility

In the planning phase of a project, specific project goals and requirements are defined. These goals and requirements are broken down into the specific steps and tasks necessary for completion of these goals and requirements in the statement of work and responsibility. It is a detailed project plan, including specific tasks, assignment of responsibility for those tasks, the time and resources required for the tasks, target start and completion dates, and task interdependencies. In the case of computer software implementation, the statement of work and responsibility is organized according to the modules and sub-modules available for use.

Advantages of Utilizing Network Scheduling Methods

Network scheduling methods are tools that aid in project planning. Examples of network scheduling methods are Gantt charts, the critical path method (CPM), and the program evaluation and review technique (PERT). These typically computerized methods provide clear and logical planning, scheduling that clearly specifies both flexible and critical target dates, optimization of resource allocation due to the categorization of flexible and critical targets, project progress tracking and the resulting accountability and control, and clear visual communication to all team members of what needs to be accomplished, when, and by whom.

Project Planning Terms

- Gantt chart: A network scheduling method in which project tasks are plotted against time, tracking the target task start dates, end dates, duration, and ongoing progress and linking interdependent tasks.
- Critical path method (CPM): A network scheduling method in which project tasks are visually depicted according to their interrelationship and tagged with time required for completion to form a critical path, the shortest time possible for project completion and identification of critical tasks in which delays would set back the overall project completion time.
- Program evaluation and review technique (PERT): A network scheduling method in which project tasks are visually depicted according to their interrelationship and tagged with best case, worst case, and probable completion times to determine the most likely project completion time and identify critical tasks in which delays would set back the overall project completion time.

Critical Path Method

Producing the network of activities for the critical path method requires detailing the project steps, documenting the dependencies between them, and forming the network diagram. Arrows are drawn representing the activities to be completed, with circles as nodes between the arrows. The activities are mapped in order of dependencies, with parallel branches forming as required. Inside the node circles, the stages are numbered and start and end dates are recorded. The path through the nodes without floats is critical. Floats are slack time caused by parallel paths of different time lengths. The shorter path is not critical since the length of time required by the longer path is available for completion. The longer path is critical since delays there delay the whole project. The network diagram can be utilized and distributed to affected personnel as is, or it can be converted into a schedule with start and completion dates before distribution. The clarification of timing and critical events helps significantly in effective resource allocation and timely project completion.

Resource and Budgetary Considerations in the Project Planning Process

Projects require resources of finance and personnel. Since the typical company does not maintain unused workers and finances, completion of a special project can require juggling of limited people and funds, while still maintaining regular work. Staffing issues can be addressed through overtime or utilizing salaried workers to complete the project in addition to their regular work. Another alternative is to hire new workers, but this must be done in a timely fashion since new workers are not typically helpful in an improvement project. The new workers must be hired and trained to perform the regular work, releasing more experienced workers to carry out the project. Initial project planning includes budgeting, but actual expenses often exceed budgeted expenses. This is an urgent problem to be handled by the executive steering committee if it arises.

Development Concepts

The following product development concepts:

- Design for manufacturability: A product design and development strategy in which manufacturing issues are considered in the original design and throughout development with particular attention given to standardization and simplification, minimizing manufacturing problems to be resolved after the design stage
- Design for quality: A product design and development strategy in which quality issues are considered in the original design and throughout development, minimizing quality problems to be resolved after the design stage
- Concurrent product development: A product design and development strategy in which all company functions and even suppliers and customers participate in the design and development of new products to meet the needs of internal and external customers while bringing the product to market quickly with maximum quality and minimum cost; concurrent product development is also referred to as concurrent engineering, participative design and participative engineering, and includes personnel from marketing, sales, design and development, manufacturing, logistics, and more simultaneously
- Quality function deployment (QFD): A product design and development strategy focusing on identification and fulfillment of customer requirements through translating the voice of the customer (VOC) into technical terms and communicating those requirements to all staff with design input; QFD is closely associated with house of quality

- Standardization and simplification: A product design and development strategy used to design for manufacturability as well as eliminate time, process, and part waste in manufacturing through such practices as common routings, standardized production methods, consistent process cycle times (to avoid work in progress and queuing), minimization and commonality of parts used, factory synchronization, design and development based on existing components, reduction of complexity in operations, and more

Design Process

The design and development process employed by a company has a direct impact on operations and the company's execution of its strategic plan. Time, cost, and quality are critical factors in achieving and maintaining competitiveness and profitability. Cost and time to market can be minimized through integrated or participative design in place of traditional or sequential design and development, and through materials standardization and manufacturing simplification. The product's quality level and design must be sufficient to meet market demand and compare favorably with or even surpass the competition. The concept of customer focus can help a company reach this standard of design and quality.

Process Design

Process design is the development of manufacturing operations for a new product, specifically determining the manufacturing methods and location within the factory to be used. The product routing, inventory flow, capacity utilization, and cycle time are all set through process design. The critical objectives of process design to ensure profitability and competitiveness are minimization of throughput time, simplification of operations, and process support for the customer quality level, product mix, and flexibility required. Production engineers work in conjunction with manufacturing supervisors and operators to develop the process and contribute expertise in tool design, equipment modification, set-up reduction, layout changes, and scrap reduction. In a just-in-time (JIT) manufacturing environment, inexpensive, flexible equipment is preferred to expensive, inflexible equipment. Tool design and redesign are performed with the goals of quick setups and changeovers and repeatable precision.

Role of Cycle Time, Stable Production Rates, and Process Improvement in Process Design

Manufacturing cycle time is closely associated with lead time, so the shorter it is the better. Longer cycle times cause slower responsiveness to market demand. Ideally, the cycle time pattern should be smooth and regular, creating steady pacing of supply and production. Synchronization is an important factor. Synchronized processing, where one operation flows directly into the next, eliminates queuing and minimizes inventory. Since queuing is typically the largest time component of cycle time, reducing it significantly reduces the cycle time, increasing market responsiveness and thus competitiveness.

Regardless of the production environment or the nature of the business, a stable production rate is necessary to maintain flexibility. The rate can change, but there must be periods of stability.

Effective process improvement requires thorough understanding of the current process, which can be achieved through developing a process flow chart. First, non-essential activities should be identified and eliminated rather than improved. The goal of process improvement after eliminating non-essential activities is to determine and resolve the issues causing poor quality and process variation.

Terms of Routing, Manufacturing Instruction, and Flow

- Routing: A product's pathway through manufacturing, including the manufacturing operations to be performed, the sequence of those operations, the equipment or work centers and methods to be used, and the tooling, length of time, and grade of labor required; routing information is recorded in the routing file and sometimes additional information is available in the associated manufacturing instruction.
- Routing file: The record of a product's routing, also called the route sheet, including the operation numbers, work centers, descriptions of processes, set-up time and specifications, unit run time, labor grades, and any specialized information required by the industry or company.
- Manufacturing instruction: Detailed operator instructions for a process specified in the route sheet; manufacturing instructions are provided along with the route sheets.
- Inventory flow: A process design strategy in which inventory is minimized by decreasing or eliminating work in process, queuing, and other causes of idle products and materials.
- Capacity utilization: A process design strategy focusing on balanced utilization of machinery so that bottlenecks do not occur and steady flow is maintained through manufacturing; traditionally, the ideal capacity utilization has been 80%, but is now as low as 60% to maximize customer responsiveness and customer service level and reduce inventory.
- Flow process chart: A table or chart depicting the sequence of activities and operations in a manufacturing process, including all specific actions performed during operations and between operations, the time required for each action, the distances the product is moved for processing, and categorization of actions as value adding or non-value adding; flow charts are used to understand and analyze a process, particularly whether steps are value-adding or non-value adding.

Design, Development and Cost Management

Although design and development and cost management processes are not actually a part of operations, they have a significant impact on the effectiveness of operations. Design and development entails exploring and evaluating concepts, transforming concepts into products, and designing the actual products and their corresponding processes. Design and development feeds the products to be manufactured and the processes through which they are produced into operations. Cost management involves recording, organizing, and storing data like financial results, asset valuations, operational control, and product costing for the purpose of informing the decision-making process. The decisions made through cost management affect ongoing operations as well as the company's competitiveness.

Product Closeout

The final phase of a project is closeout, in which project tasks are finalized and the successful fulfillment of project goals and requirements is verified. Task completion, benefit verification, and customer agreement, among other things, are included in the closeout process. Task completion involves certifying that all activities have been performed. The project team members each do this for their own area of responsibility, and the project manager does it for general tasks. Since the expected benefits to be provided by a project are a major part of the decision to pursue it, successful closeout requires verifying that those benefits are being reaped, or are well on their way to being reaped. Otherwise, the project is not completed. Customer agreement for closeout is essential when customer agreement was part of the justification or motivation for the project. The customer must agree that requirements are being met and benefits received from their perspective.

The final phase of a project is closeout, in which project tasks are finalized and the successful fulfillment of project goals and requirements is verified. User documentation, project documentation, and audit, among other things, are included in the closeout process. User documentation refers to the formal materials developed by the project team for later education and training of system users. This can take the form of manuals or system training modules. The training modules are usually more practical and easier to maintain as changes occur. Project documentation is the record of what transpired in the project for future reference. The project justification, requirements, budget, agreements, project plan with updates, and meeting minutes are all included. An ongoing audit of the system should be developed and implemented with specific assessment points to check that the system is still being used and maintained as intended.

Overhead Cost Rate

The following steps for determining the overhead cost rate:

- Estimation of indirect costs: The assessment of general work center costs which are not attributable to particular jobs performed or goods produced, such as utilities, communication, and management
- Allocation of non-productive costs: The assignment of non-productive costs like employee benefits and non-specific material costs to specific work centers, usually based on the relationship between the non-productive costs and the work center in question
- Calculation of overhead costs: The determination of an overhead charge rate for a work center by dividing the total overhead cost (the sum of estimated indirect costs and allocated non-productive costs) by the predicted activity level for the work center
- Allocation of overhead costs: The assignment of overhead costs to individual items produced based on the overhead charge rate and labor or equipment capacity utilized to produce the given item

Cost Accounting Methods

The following manufacturing cost accounting methods:

- Standard costing: A manufacturing costing system based on predetermined target or theoretical costs for operations and materials; discrepancies between actual and standard costs are recorded and maintained in a variance account; the advantage of standard costing is cost stabilization so that production management and sell price determination are simplified; standard costs have traditionally been set yearly, but are now usually set quarterly
- Process costing: A manufacturing costing system in which total production costs for a time period are tracked and averaged per unit produced in that time period, using equivalent units of production
- Equivalent unit of production: The amount of work required to process one typical manufacturing unit; equivalent units of production are used as a common base among items being processed; work in process (WIP) is estimated to be 50% complete, and atypical items are assigned a fraction or multiple of equivalent units to quantify work performed
- Project costing: A manufacturing costing method used in production of major specialized assignments built in response to customer orders, such as buildings, bridges, or ships, in which the total cost of the assignment is tracked until completed using actual or standard costs
- Actual costing: A manufacturing costing system in which the costs incurred in production are tracked as they occur, both direct and indirect costs, and attributed to products manufactured

- Activity-based costing (ABC): A recently developed manufacturing costing system in which costs are tracked according to cost-incurring actions and attributed to products, customers, or projects according to cost drivers in order to more realistically allocate overhead costs
- Cost driver: A manufacturing function or activity unrelated to specific operations or products that requires workload and/or effort and thus incurs cost, such as purchasing, quality assurance, and engineering change notes; cost drivers are used to allocate costs to the activity they belong to, and are useful for process improvement since activity costs and status as value-adding or non-value-adding can be easily gauged
- Technology accounting: A recently developed manufacturing costing system in which overhead costs for products are determined by the equipment rather than the labor that is utilized in production in order to quantify more accurate overhead costs in situations where equipment and technology depreciation are significant and cannot be effectively averaged or ignored

How the Manufacturing Environment Impacts the Manufacturing Cost Accounting Method Utilized

The system(s) of manufacturing costing employed in a given situation is based on the volume of goods produced and the manufacturing process utilized. In most situations, some form of standard or process costing is used, with process costing being reserved for homogenous, high-volume, process environments like in oil refineries or chemical plants. Project costing is used for substantial, one-time, made-to-order assignments like bridges, buildings, or capital equipment. More recent project costing innovations are activity-based costing (ABC) and technology accounting. ABC attributes costs to manufacturing functions and activities and technology accounting bases overhead costs on equipment used, both in an effort to more accurately apportion costs than the traditional methods do.

Standard Costs

Standard costs, or the predetermined theoretical production costs upon which standard costing is based, are calculated as follows: determine the current actual total cost for manufacturing, set the time period for which the standard cost is applicable (usually a quarter), estimate the actual total cost of production at the end of the period, and average the starting and ending manufacturing costs per item to calculate the standard cost. As production occurs, the actual costs incurred are tracked and compared to the standard costs so that discrepancies between the two can be accounted for and future calculated standard costs can be adjusted as necessary.

Assets

The following terms of assets:

- Assets: All of a company's resources, including its inventory, equipment, facilities, and property; assets can be fixed or current.
- Asset valuation: The assignment of monetary value to a company's assets or resources, for accounting purpose.
- Fixed assets: Resources that last and are utilized by the company long-term, such as buildings and manufacturing equipment; some fixed assets such as machinery decrease in value from the time of purchase, and this depreciation is based on government tax guidelines or estimation of the machine's useful life span and attributed to factory overhead costs.
- Current assets: Fluid resources quickly converted into cash such as debts owed to the company or accounts receivable, inventory, and cash on hand.

Projects

A project is the organized and purposeful accomplishment of a stated goal within a controlled timeline and budget. Project management is the overarching activity of identifying, selecting, planning, and executing projects, or solutions to problems or improvements to products and/or processes, including analysis of the status quo and identification of the target and the means to go from the first to the latter. The project life cycle is the process of completing a project from beginning to end, including planning, implementation, and closing phases. Projects are initially evaluated based on the resources, time, and cost required, balanced with the expected benefit to be achieved from the project.

Three Phases of a Project Life Cycle

The first phase of a project life cycle is planning. Planning a project includes identification of the project goals, required personnel, timeline, and budget, which are further broken down into specific tasks to be performed during implementation and individual responsibility and time deadlines for these tasks. Management approval of the plan is required before implementation. A good plan makes implementation easier.

The second phase of a project life cycle is implementation. Implementing the plan is the bulk of the work, and entails acquiring necessary resources, establishing new operating methods, monitoring progress, training affected personal as necessary, and executing any other planned or required tasks. Implementation may be multi-phased if the project is large and/or complex, and management must be kept informed of progress.

The last phase of a project life cycle is closing. Closing includes verification of completed objectives and formally ending the project, specifically completing all associated tasks, gaining management and customer approval, finalizing documentation, and conducting a close-out meeting for all staff involved and affected.

Roles in Project Organization

- Executive steering committee: An upper level management team responsible for setting the project scope and priorities and providing the necessary resources
- Change champion: An upper level staff member responsible for generating project acceptance and support throughout the company
- Project manager: The actual project leader who is accountable to the executive steering committee for the project's success; the project manager needs good people and management skills
- Project team: Representatives, preferably management, from the different departments impacted by the project, who are also responsible for the actual project work, along with any relevant specialists
- Task teams: Subordinates to the project team members to whom specific tasks can be delegated by the project team members
- Users/customers: The key people impacted by the project who are responsible for fully testing the new or modified system and identifying any problems or potential problems

Product Profile

The product profile is the volume and variety of products to be produced in a facility. This product range and volume determine the type of manufacturing environment needed: job shop, batch manufacturing, line manufacturing, or continuous manufacturing. In a job shop environment, material stocking is based on replenishment or requirements planning, but material issues are made only in response to manufacturing orders. The individual manufacturing orders are scheduled and then tracked through processing so that completion dates are met. In a batch manufacturing environment, material stocking is based on requirements planning. Material is released into production in response to a manufacturing order or as replenishment is needed when a back flushing scheme is in effect. Material is produced in response to scheduled manufacturing orders, and must be tracked to assure timely completion. A kanban system can also be used.

In line manufacturing, material is stocked according to a "schedule the vendor" method or a release system, and typically delivered to the point of use and counted through back flushing. Repetitive line manufacturing proceeds according to a schedule, and products with options are completed in response to a manufacturing order. In continuous manufacturing, material is delivered to the point of use and counted by back flushing. Manufacturing is driven completely by schedule, with production reported at predetermined checkpoints or the point of storage.

Master Production Schedule

The master scheduler is responsible for converting the quantities and timing set in top-level management's production plan into a master production schedule (MPS), taking into account lead times required for materials acquisition and production of goods. The purpose of the MPS, generally, is to enable the manufacturing function to fulfill its role in the company's strategic plan. The MPS accomplishes this by providing a detailed manufacturing plan, facilitating the material planning at all levels necessary to meet the plan, allowing verification of balanced workloads to meet the plan, and providing the "available-to-promise" facility to customer orders. It is a specific blueprint to help manufacturing meet the more general strategy.

Effect of the Product Profile

In a job shop environment, the MPS is based on typical or average requirements. In batch manufacturing, the end items produced are scheduled in the MPS in the traditional way using demand forecasts. Line manufacturing requires scheduling of items on the MPS at the option level, rather than the end item level, when options are available. Scheduling may also be based on product run rates. Continuous manufacturing differs from the others in that the MPS details product run rates, rather than the traditional scheduling of product volume.

Material Requirements Planning

Material requirements planning (MRP) is the process of breaking down the master production schedule (MPS), which details the volume and variety of products to be manufactured per time period, into all component parts and raw materials necessary for production, and assuring that those items are available when they are needed for manufacturing the finished goods by the MPS time deadlines. Through MRP, material shortages are avoided or reduced, and orders (both internal and external) are kept prioritized. MRP uses a reverse logic, beginning with the MPS end requirement and working backward to determine what will be needed when to meet production goals.

Effect of the Product Profile

In a job shop environment, MRP is initially based on typical or average bills of material, which are ultimately replaced by actual customer bills of material for detailed final planning and manufacture. In batch manufacturing, the MRP is based on standard, multi-level bills of material of end items required by the MPS in the traditional way. Repetitive line manufacturing requires traditional MRP based on MPS product requirements. Line manufacturing with a final assembly schedule (FAS) to allow customer options requires MRP for subassemblies, which are later finalized according to the FAS based on customer orders. MRP in continuous manufacturing environments is based on the product run rate required by the MPS.

Operations Management Execution

Operations management execution is the means by which the operations management planning is executed by fulfilling the material plan. There are two primary functions, purchasing execution (procurement) and manufacturing execution. Execution of the material plan in manufacturing can occur either through production activity control (PAC) or kanban. Procurement can be accomplished through traditional purchase orders, standing purchase orders like the release system, or supplier partnerships. PAC is the group of mechanisms used to control the volume and priority of work in manufacturing. Kanban is a simple part replacement system, in which parts are replaced as they are used. Kanban replenishment is driven by actual demand or use rather than by a schedule. Kanban can be used along with or instead of PAC.

Production Activity Control System

The role of a production activity control (PAC) system is to provide the information needed by manufacturing planners and managers to make and implement decisions in day-to-day manufacturing. The essential functions of a PAC system include the detailed scheduling of manufacturing operations, both start and completion dates, as well as the actual loading of the operations on the manufacturing floor through work orders, manufacturing instruction sheets, routing sheets, dispatching and more. Tracking the movement of goods through processing and reporting production information are also key, so that work in process can be monitored and order status, work center efficiency, machine utilization, etc. are known. Recording of additional information such as worker attendance for payroll purposes or regulatory data may also be needed by the specific industry and company in question.

Appraisal, Compensation, and Recognition

Appraisal, compensation, and recognition as they relate to appraisal and reward systems:

- Appraisal: An assessment or rating of job performance or progress toward predetermined job-related goals; historically, a simple check of whether or not the employee reached a specified target required to earn a reward; a discussion between an employee and management centered on identifying an employee's strengths and weaknesses, the expected improvement, and the opportunities and training provided by the company to foster improvement
- Compensation: The payment received by an employee for the work performed, usually hourly; compensation recognizes and rewards the quantity of the work performed; the method of compensation varies
- Recognition: The acknowledgement received by an employee for effort made in performing the job, recognizing the quality rather than quantity of the work performed; recognition is an important tool in motivating and building self-esteem in employees

Approaches to Compensation

The four general methods of compensation are incentives, fixed rates, skills-based rates, and profit sharing. There are many variations of the incentive method, but all involve payment made to workers for work that is accomplished. Individual and gang piecework are two examples. An individual working alone or a group working together receives payment, individually or corporately, respectively, for the number of items produced. Fixed rates encompass the practice of paying workers for their time, usually hourly, rather than for work accomplished. Skills-based rates encourage worker flexibility. Workers are given the opportunity to expand their skills, and their pay is based on the amount, classification, and difficulty of skills acquired. Profit sharing includes many types of program whereby employee compensation is linked to company profits. This practice encourages continuous company improvement by all workers at all levels.

Compensation-Based Reward Systems

Employee compensation methodologies include fixed rate, incentive, skills based, and profit sharing frameworks. Within the fixed rate system, employees are simply compensated for the time worked, while the other systems reward the employee in some way for work accomplished. In these methods, incentive, skills-based, and profit sharing, performance measures are tied into the reward the employee receives for work performed. The incentive method is an inhibiting performance measure since it promotes competition at the cost of cooperation and teamwork and encourages production at all times, even if it is not necessary for meeting goals. Skills based employee compensation encourages flexibility, and profit sharing encourages ownership, teamwork, and cooperation among employees, so these are enabling performance measures.

Enablers and Inhibitors

The purpose of performance measurements is to establish a baseline for performance and to track ongoing improvement and/or deterioration from there and respond accordingly. Good performance measurements correlate well to the manufacturing strategy and production environment in use, are not limited to financial considerations, provide accurate and timely feedback that is easily understood by all personnel, are continually revised to function better, and are conducive to making improvements. Enablers are performance measurements that encourage product and process improvements, while inhibitors are performance measurements that encourage actions and attitudes in opposition to the established goals.

Enabling Performance Measurements

- Value added per employment dollar: A performance measurement in which the portion of labor wages and salaries paid that actually add value to the products manufactured is calculated, expressed as value added per dollar spent; the value added per employment dollar increases as waste decreases
- Parts per million defects: A performance measurement in which the number of observed defective parts per million parts processed is tracked; the parts per million defects decreases as quality increases, particularly as total quality management is introduced
- Throughput-based performance measures: Performance measurements in which the production output rate is tracked; throughput-based performance measurements improve as processing waste is eliminated
- Cost of quality: A performance measurement in which the costs incurred by the company to produce goods of the required quality level are tracked; the cost of quality decreases as just-in-time (JIT) manufacturing and total quality management (TQM) techniques are effectively introduced
- Total cost of material acquisition: A performance measurement in which the costs incurred to acquire materials are tracked; the total cost of material acquisition decreases as process improvements are made to lower material costs besides the purchase price, such as placing, receiving, and storing orders
- Shipment linearity: A performance measurement in which the number of shipments made are tracked at regular time intervals within the time period, usually daily; shipment linearity should even out as process improvements are made to remove manufacturing variation
- Trends vs. absolutes: A performance measurement in which not only the actual values of relevant data but also the trends of those data over time are tracked to observe process shifting and tendencies that warrant improvement

- Velocity: A performance measurement in which the rate or speed at which manufacturing output is produced is measured and tracked; the velocity increases as the time required for production decreases as waste is removed from manufacturing processes
- Number of kanbans: A performance measurement in which the quantity of kanban refills made is recorded and tracked; the number of kanban refills should decrease as manufacturing improvements are made to decrease manufacturing variation

Inhibiting Performance Measurements

- Purchase price: A performance measurement in which the price paid directly for raw materials and components for manufacturing is tracked; purchase price alone as a performance measurement is an inhibitor since the quality and delivery timeliness of acquired goods are more important than price in meeting company goals; the total cost of material acquisition, which includes quality and delivery considerations, is the corresponding enabler
- Variance: A performance measurement in which production output of individual manufacturing workers is tracked and compared to the manufacturing plan; variance can act as an inhibitor since individual performance measurements can encourage competition and frustrate cooperative improvements efforts aimed at making continuous small improvements
- Utilization: A performance measurement in which the extent of use of manufacturing equipment or work centers is monitored; utilization as a performance measurement is an inhibitor since increased utilization requires greater use which can result in unnecessary production; utilization information can be important for other uses, but work center or equipment performance to plan is the corresponding enabling performance measurement
- Efficiency: A performance measurement in which the actual production output for a worker, machine or work center is tracked and compared to the expected output for given time periods or input materials; efficiency as a performance measurement is an inhibitor since it encourages specialization and discourages worker cross training and flexibility; also, individual measurements encourage competition and discourage working together to meet company goals
- Defects per person: A performance measurement in which production output of individual workers is inspected to determine the number of defects; defects per person as a performance measurement is an inhibitor since it interferes with just-in-time manufacturing practices where material flows from one worker to the next and workers immediately identify, communicate and resolve defects; also, individual measurements encourage competition and discourage working together to meet company goals
- Overhead rates: A performance measurement in which general costs that enable manufacturing but are not attributable to specific products manufactured are tracked; overhead rate, also called burden, as a performance measurement is an inhibitor since it can encourage unnecessary production to cover overhead because it is assumed that a department's output compensates for its costs including overhead, but it is actually the sale of the department's output and not the output itself that compensates for costs

Benchmarking

Benchmarking Measures

- Inventory turns: A benchmarking measurement in which a company's number of inventory stock turns is compared to that of their competitors; care must be taken to ensure that the inventory turns are actually comparable, which they are not if there are significant process differences such as component fabrication vs. component purchase

- Employees to output ratio: A benchmarking measurement in which the ratio of a company's employees to its output is calculated and compared to competitors; care must be taken to ensure that the ratios are comparable, which they may not be if they do not perform manufacturing from the same starting point and according to the same processes and procedures
- Market share: A benchmarking measurement in which a company's portion of its industry's total sales market is calculated and compared to the portions held by its competitors

Difficulties in and Some Practical Methods for Competitive Benchmarking

Even large companies can have trouble with internal comparisons between divisions and sites when there is open information sharing because of economies of scale, local environments, and other significant factors. These factors also apply to comparisons between companies, especially when they are competitors and information is not openly shared but maintained in confidentiality. When trying to perform effective competitive benchmarking, it is important to note that trends are more important than the actual values. The actual competitor values may be impossible to discover. The central principle to embrace is that of learning from other companies. For direct competitors, this can be done through published information about the competitors themselves and the industry in general and public site visits, sometimes conducted through APICS chapters. Coming to an understanding of practices considered the industry's best is helpful. More open and detailed information exchange and learning can occur through relationships with companies in related fields but not in direct competition.

Important Terms

Strategic plan: A company's blueprint detailing its overall aim and how that aim will be accomplished.

Marketplace: The field of potential customers.

Market research: The collection and analysis of information related to marketing products and services, including market analysis, sales analysis, and consumer research.

Market analysis: The study of the marketplace itself, such as the number, location, and qualities of the potential customers.

Sales analysis: The study of sales figures to determine trends and make comparisons.

Consumer research: The study of the thoughts, feelings, and other feedback of customers of a particular industry toward that industry's products.

Competitors: Companies within the same industry trying to win the same field of customers.

Market share: The portion of the available marketplace for their product(s) that a company wins as customers.

Competitive stance: The unique position a company takes in marketing their products, differentiating them from the products of competitors.

Competitive analysis: The collection and comparison of data related to a company's marketplace and competitors, such as the market share of each competitor.

Distinctive competencies: A company's unique strengths that attract customers to buy their products; distinctive competencies function as a company's order winners.

Resolving Capacity Shortages

There are three primary ways to quickly resolve capacity shortages in production. These are increased work force levels, worker overtime, and subcontracting. Increasing work force levels simply means hiring more workers. This is especially useful if capacity is worker-related rather than machine-related, or if the machines stand idle for second or thirds shifts. Additional workers can run the machines in previously idle times. Worker overtime is similar, except it involves the same workers increasing their hours, rather than increasing hours by hiring new workers. Subcontracting is hiring another individual or company to perform manufacturing operations offsite. Worker overtime and already existing subcontracting relationships are the most immediate means available for meeting capacity shortages. Hiring and training new workers to increase the work force level and developing subcontracting relationships both require time to be done well.

Implementing Change

Project Implementation

Steps Involved in Project Implementation

Project implementation, particularly phasing in manufacturing resource planning (MRPII) or enterprise resource planning (ERP), requires many steps. The steps include first cut education for management, full course education for project team members and system users, formulation of a requirements statement, selection of a system, configuration of the system for use within the specific environment, module training for the rest of the company's staff, simulation training for the system users, a pilot run, a full run, an audit after implementation is complete, and continuous system improvement. The executive steering committee, comprised of top-level management, is responsible to establish project priorities and guidelines, provide necessary resources, require accountability for progress, establish company-wide acceptance and cooperation, and mediate conflict resolution. The executive steering committee should include the company's chief executive officer (CEO), the vice presidents of marketing/sales, finance/accounting, and manufacturing/operations, and the project manager.

- First cut education: Background training for the executive steering committee so that they can make informed project decisions.
- Full course education: Detailed training for the project team and key users to communicate principles and enhance understanding of the project being undertaken.
- Statement of requirements: Detailed guidelines for what the project should accomplish and provide for the company, often established with external help.
- System selection: The decision regarding the means of executing the project, including the selection of hardware and a particular software package or in-house software development in the case of manufacturing resource planning (MRPII).
- Configuration of system use: Developing system use within a company's particular environment, including which system functions to utilize and how.
- Module training: Specific training for personnel in how to use the new system.
- Simulation training: Training of system users through building a model of the company environment on the software and simulating actual use before implementation.
- Pilot run: Partial implementation of the system in a limited environment to verify that it will work as planned; the first step of a phased implementation.
- Full run: The actual implementation of the new system in its entirety following a successful pilot run.
- Audit: A thorough investigation and review of the system performed regularly after implementation and during ongoing use to verify that it is performing as planned, the requirements are being met, predicted benefits are materializing, and it is being used as intended; the audit is followed by troubleshooting if necessary.
- Continuous improvement: The ongoing resolution of system problems to enhance system performance.

Project Managers

The project manager is fully responsible for project execution, including serving as the liaison between the executive steering committee and the project team, management of and conflict resolution within the project team, maintenance of an up-to-date project plan, education of the project team and end users, and motivation of the end users in relation to the project. People mistakenly chosen as project managers include systems personnel, since this precludes ownership by the using department; outsiders and newcomers, since they are unfamiliar with the products, processes, and politics involved and have not yet gained the respect of their colleagues; and staff only partially dedicated to the project, since this makes completion more difficult. The project manager should have excellent interpersonal skills and a strong ability to accomplish.

Project Team Members

The project team members should be the department managers of all departments affected by the project, along with any business analysts or other specialists deemed necessary. For the department managers, serving as project team members is not a full-time task, but it is still best if they delegate a good portion of their regular responsibilities while serving on the team. They will also delegate the actual project work to subordinates within their respective departments, the project task teams. The role of project team members is to perform project-related planning, organization, decision-making, management, reporting, and training in conjunction with and as directed by the project manager. Together, the project manager and project team implement the plan and priorities set by the executive steering committee.

Project Evaluation and Selection

A wide range of projects is possible within a company at any given time. The potential projects should be assessed for costs to be incurred, benefits to be reaped, and their relationships to the company's strategic plan and order winning strategy. Project proposals should include expected financial and other benefits, anticipated costs, timing of required funding, and length of time for the investment to be recouped. All of these items should be thoroughly justified in the proposal. Actual project selection goes beyond these considerations to include project interdependencies, trade-offs, and the company's financial position.

Project Investment Analysis

In the past, potential projects were analyzed through purely financial means. Projects were selected for implementation based primarily on the cost incurred and the expected financial returns through calculating the payback and breakeven points. In the current manufacturing environment, it is understood that non-financial considerations can be just as important. Projects require three main types of investment: technology, data transformation, and personnel. Technology investment entails the cost of all necessary software and hardware, as well as software and/or hardware modifications that may be necessary. Data investment refers to the cost of transforming the company's data and data gathering and processing mechanisms into the format, accuracy and security required for the new system. Personnel investment is comprised of consultant fees and wages and salaries for the internal workers involved in the project. The financial investment required for projects can be substantial.

Project Investment Analysis Tools

- Payback method: An investment analysis tool in which the length of time required to recover the initial financial investment is estimated by dividing the initial investment by the annual net income generated by the project
- Average return on investment: An investment analysis tool in which the length of time required for the initial financial investment to be recovered from project revenue is estimated by dividing the project revenue for a set time period, usually determined in relation to the useful life of the project, by the initial cost of the investment

- Net present value method: An investment analysis tool in which the present value of future project revenue is calculated and compared to the required initial investment; the net present value is calculated by multiplying the future income by the applicable interest factor to determine its current value; projects for which the present value is greater than the required investment are considered viable
- Hurdle rate: The lowest feasible return for a project to be considered viable

The Non-Financial Considerations When Evaluating Potential Projects

The non-financial ramifications of potential projects can be more important than the straightforward financial cost and benefit analyses. Such concepts as order qualifiers, order winners, strategic drivers, competitive advantage, company strategy, and company market position must be considered in the evaluation of potential projects. How and whether the project supports these is a critical component in project selection. Even if the project does support these, it must still be considered whether a particular project is the best way to accomplish the project goal. It is also a good idea to reconsider the company's plan and related strategies in light of the current market situation to avoid making large investments based on obsolete information.

Product Quality Measurements

Product quality measurements refer to the verification of the quality level of incoming materials, work in process, or manufactured goods through inspection. The quality of the goods is not improved but rather checked. Through nondestructive testing, the good products can be sorted from the bad, and the bad products are either reworked or scrapped. A representative sample size can also be measured to determine if the batch meets the acceptable quality level (AQL). This is especially helpful in destructive testing. When product quality measurements reveal an ongoing manufacturing process problem, there must be procedures in place to respond by ascertaining and correcting the problem.

Process Quality Measurements

Process quality measurements refer to the verification of the manufacturing process. When the process is functioning correctly, then the products manufactured will be of acceptable quality, within the required specification. If the process is drifting or otherwise deteriorating, action is taken to remedy the problem. The standard method of process quality measurement is statistical process control, but other methods include product and process changeover times, production lead time, the number of process steps, the number of parts produced per machine, the number of parts used per product, and excess capacity available.

Performance Measurement

Performance measurement is a critical tool in manufacturing in general and in successfully implementing change in particular. Performance measurement reveals if the anticipated progress is being made and what changes need to occur. There are many kinds of performance measurements: financial/non-financial, local/global, productivity/process, quality, delivery speed/delivery reliability, and volume flexibility/product mix flexibility. To be successful, performance measurements must correspond to the company's strategic plan, order qualifiers, order winners, and strategic drivers. Additionally, the data recording and communication must be financially feasible, meaningful and applicable to the workers and the process, clear and timely in presentation, and relatable to a clear target so improvement can be monitored.

Baseline and Benchmark Measurements

The purpose of baseline measurements is to establish the existing level for a product, process, or company. It is an informational starting point, from which changes can be made and tracked.

These measurements occur before changes are undertaken to better understand the starting point. The purpose of benchmark measurements is to understand the level of improvement that is feasible and/or necessary. Typically, benchmark measurements are based on comparison of a product, process, or company to its competitors or industry standard. Benchmark measurements occur before changes are undertaken to establish the end goal of the change. Special care must be taken to ensure that the comparisons made in benchmarking are valid. The baseline establishes the starting point, while the benchmark establishes the target ending point.

NEGATIVE IMPACT OF POOR PERFORMANCE MEASUREMENTS

Good performance measurements reinforce the desired product, process, and/or company results. The measurements must be paired well with the desired results to be effective. Some traditional performance measurements that can negatively impact desired results include financial measurements and volume/output measures like individual incentives, machine utilization, and labor efficiency. All of these methods encourage and reward overproduction, at the expense of other important factors like quality, customer service, reliability, and flexibility. Financial measurements, particularly management accounting reports, reveal problems too late and do not pinpoint the nature or source of the problems. Individual production incentives are problematic because they bear no relationship to demand and product quality. Machine utilization measurements discourage repair, maintenance, and upkeep of equipment since the downtime required lowers performance. Labor efficiency measurements discourage flexibility.

MANUFACTURING PERFORMANCE MEASUREMENTS

Work center performance data such as cost, efficiency, utilization, and performance to schedule are necessary for good production management, future planning, and identification of needed improvements. Since the workers respond to measurements, it is crucial that the combination of measurements taken actually reinforces the desired results. For example, performance to schedule is a better measurement than utilization alone, since utilization statistics can encourage overproduction and poor quality. Some major manufacturing performance measurements include productivity, throughput time, product quality, and process quality. Additional measurements that may be utilized include product and process changeover times, number of steps per process, range of goods manufactured, number of parts per product, and excess capacity.

PRODUCTIVITY AND THROUGHPUT TIME

Productivity is the capability to produce a good or provide a service. It is measured by comparing the input materials and/or labor to the production output. Productivity can be calculated in two ways. First, productivity is the product of the efficiency and utilization. Alternatively, productivity is the ratio of standard hours required for a task to the scheduled labor time. The result of both calculations is the same.

Throughput time is defined two ways. It is the length of time between the completion of two manufacturing units, or it is the length of time between the entry of production materials into a factory and the exit of goods built from those materials from the factory. Throughput time is measured directly, not calculated.

Measuring throughput time implies the desire or need to reduce it. Throughput time and lead time are closely linked, so this performance measurement is often used as a tool in reducing lead time. Lead time reduction is the premise of just in time (JIT) manufacturing, a manufacturing philosophy espousing waste reduction in machinery, materials, space, labor and time. Specifically, JIT is implemented and throughput time is reduced through setup, lead time, queue size, and lot size reduction. Decreasing setup shortens throughput time and decreases minimum lot sizes. Lead time reduction decreases work in process (WIP), increases flexibility, and adds accuracy to forecasting. Lead times are measured to track progress in reducing them as well as to gauge the accuracy of standard lead times. Large queues decrease the company's ability to perform to schedule. The most economic manufacturing batch size is one, although this is generally not feasible because of issues like setup.

QUALITY

QUALITY ISSUE TERMS

- Quality: The grade or level of product or service excellence; a product or service's level of conformance to its required characteristics or its fitness for use
- Quality assurance: The quality function of building excellence, usability, specified requirements and more into a product or service; the prevention of product or service defects
- Quality control: The quality function of testing or inspecting products and/or services for their level of quality, and eliminating those deemed defective; the detection of product or service defects
- Conformance quality: The extent to which a product or service meets its required characteristics and/or specifications; good conformance quality implies the absence of specified, measurable defects from the product or service
- Acceptable quality level (AQL): A tool for measuring the conformance quality of a batch of goods based on sampling the batch to verify that the percentage of defective goods is lower than the established limit

QUALITY ASSURANCE AND QUALITY CONTROL AS THEY RELATE TO ACCEPTABLE QUALITY LEVELS (AQL'S)

The acceptable quality level (AQL) is a tool for measuring a representative sample from a batch of goods (or the whole batch, if the testing is nondestructive) to determine if the percentage of the batch that is defective is below the established limit, and accepting or rejecting the batch to be used in manufacturing or sold to customers accordingly. AQL is actually a quality control technique, since it is used to test the quality of goods after they have been produced. Quality assurance, however, is the process of verifying that the goods will be of acceptable quality through structuring operations to produce to the required level. Quality assurance aids in the production of goods that will pass the test, and can even make the testing unnecessary.

COST, FAILURE AND PREVENTION

- Cost of quality: The money spent on preventing and detecting product or service defects throughout the production process, from design until final sales and beyond; quality costs can be divided into four categories: internal failures, external failures, appraisal costs, and prevention costs
- Internal failure costs: Expenses resulting from product defects that appear before the product is sold to the customer causing rework and additional testing and inspection as well as product scrap and process loss
- External failures: Expenses resulting from product defects that appear after the customer has purchased the product causing warranty and return transactions
- Appraisal costs: Expenses resulting from evaluating quality such as inspections, tests, calibrations, and quality audits
- Prevention costs: Expenses resulting from quality improvement and appraisal reduction activities such as personnel education and training and supplier certification

Minimizing Quality Costs

In a good quality system, the aim for the total cost of quality should be prevention costs and minimized appraisal costs. The goal for internal and external failures costs is zero. Money should be invested in appraisal and prevention activities to undercut expenses due to internal and external failures. Process improvements and product testing can prevent costly internal and external failures. Additionally, money invested in prevention activities can undercut appraisal expenses. Supplier certification eliminates the need for incoming AQL testing for certified suppliers. Quality costs cannot be eliminated, but they can be minimized through proactive quality spending.

Designing for Quality

Designing for quality is a multi-disciplinary approach to the design process. Design, process, quality, marketing and other personnel are part of the design process from the beginning. In this way, a design is developed that meets customer desires and quality requirements and is easy to produce. When the product is designed by the engineers, then handed off to manufacturing for process development, then handed off to quality for gauging specifications, and so on, the result is a long, inefficient process resulting in a less than optimal product, manufacturing process, and quality. Quality must be built into the design from the beginning to achieve the best result.

Quality at the Source

Quality at the source is a total quality management (TQM) concept based on the material supplier or producer's responsibility to provide parts of impeccable quality to the next operation in the manufacturing flow. This includes the feeding of goods from suppliers to their customers as well as internally from process to process and worker to worker. Quality at the source depends upon thorough and effective job training, immediate performance feedback, worker self-inspection, availability of appropriate work tools, worker self-accountability, worker authority to resolve problems, assistance to external suppliers in defect reduction informally or through supplier certification, and scrap reduction. Quality at the source reduces appraisal, internal failure and external failure costs.

Inventory

The following inventory terms:

- Perpetual inventory recording: A method of inventory accounting in which stock records are kept up-to-date at all times by recording all inventory transactions as they occur
- Periodic inventory recording: A method of inventory accounting in which individual transactions are not recorded, but periodic counts are performed; periodic inventory accounting is not suitable for large organizations or in complex manufacturing since accurate current inventory balances are required, and periodic inventory recording balances are only as up-to-date as the last count
- Inventory valuation: The assignment of financial value to inventory, including the purchase price of raw materials and components, the cost of ordering and receiving raw those materials and components, and applicable labor and overhead costs.

Inventory Valuation Methods

- Last in first out (LIFO): An inventory valuation method in which the most recently received inventory is released from inventory first and valued at its actual cost and the older presumably less expensive stock is left in storage, requiring meticulous recording of inventory values and resulting in quick impact of inflation or deflation on production costs.

- First in first out (FIFO): An inventory valuation method in which goods in inventory are released from inventory in the same order that they were received into inventory and valued at their actual cost, so the older, presumably less expensive material is used first and the newer, presumably more expensive material remains in storage, requiring meticulous recording of inventory values and resulting in slow impact of inflation or deflation on production costs.
- Weighted moving average: An inventory valuation method in which all goods stored are valued at their average cost and order of release from inventory is inconsequential; with the weighted moving average recordkeeping is simplified since individual values are not necessary, and the effect of inflation and deflation on production costs is smoothed out; the weighted moving average is calculated by adding the total cost of new items deposited into inventory to the total cost of current inventory and dividing by the number of new and current inventory items.
- Latest price: An inventory valuation method in which all inventory of a particular item is valued at the latest purchase price for that item, regardless of the actual purchase price paid for the inventory; recordkeeping of inventory values is simplified, and sales will generate enough money to replace raw materials.
- Standard costing: An inventory valuation method in which a predetermined theoretical value is set and used for inventory in a given time period; actual costs are also tracked for the time period and records of variances between the standard and actual costs are maintained.
- Actual costing: An inventory valuation method used in conjunction with lot control in which the inventory is valued at its actual cost, which cost is then associated with the particular manufacturing batch in which the inventory is used.
- Replacement costing: An inventory valuation method in which the inventory is valued at the cost that would be incurred in replacing it; replacement costing is generally used for machinery.

Inventory Write-Off

In accounting, the inventory held by a company is considered to be an asset. Over time, inventory becomes obsolete, but obsolete inventory is still held in the company's accounts as assets. Holding unnecessary inventory costs the company money without any return on the investment, so the inventory should be written off and disposed of. In the period that the inventory is written off, there is a financial loss in the company's books because the inventory being written off was previously considered an asset. Unfortunately, management tends to hold on to the unnecessary inventory, wasting money on inventory holding costs, in order to record a good theoretical financial bottom line for a given period. Because of this accounting inconsistency of considering inventory an asset even when it is a liability, other methods must be used to gauge a company's profitability and credit-worthiness based on the effectiveness of its inventory management and investment. This is usually measured by calculating a company's return on their inventory investment.

Stock-Out and Service Cost

Stock-out percentage is a general, organization-wide performance measurement gauging a company's ability to respond to demand calculated as the ratio of the number of orders resulting in a stock out to the total number of orders.

Cost of service is the inventory and inventory holding costs that are incurred by a company in stocking to reach its desired customer service level or ratio. There is an exponential relationship between the customer service level and the corresponding cost of service; higher customer service levels yield higher customer satisfaction but require greater inventory and cost of service investment.

Engineering Performance Measurements

Engineering performance measurements are metrics of product design and design-related customer satisfaction. One critical engineering performance measurement in today's competitive market is time to market, the length of time from a product concept until its manufacture for the market. Analysis of the engineering change notes (ECN's), orders for engineering changes to products, can indicate the effectiveness of the design process by addressing the initial understanding of customer requirements, the understanding of manufacturing capabilities and capacities, the level of manufacturing involvement, and the level of customer communication in the design process. ECN history is an insightful tool to examine the effectiveness of the design process. Additional engineering performance measurements include the number of total components and new components utilized, the number of design changes and drawing corrections, and product recalls and warranty claims made. Through attention to engineering performance measurements a company gains understanding of the level of design and thus product quality achieved and how to improve for the future.

Sales Performance Measurements

The following sales performance measurements:

- Sales vs. quotas: A sales performance measurement in which actual sales are tracked and compared to predetermined sales quotas, in volume or value; the sales vs. quotas metric can be significant since budgets may be set according to sales quotas.
- Sales vs. forecast: A sales performance measurement in which actual sales are tracked and compared to forecast sales; the sales vs. forecast metric is feedback for forecasting personnel to determine the accuracy of their forecasts and establish why forecasts were missed and adjust future forecasts as necessary.
- Sales vs. sales plan: A sales performance measurement in which actual sales are tracked and compared to the sales plan established through sales and operation planning; the sales vs. sales plan metric is important since other manufacturing planning is derived from the sales plan.
- Number of calls made: A sales performance measurement in which the number of calls made by sales personnel per time period is tracked in relation to a specified minimum number; the number of calls metric is an accountability tool used in managing field sales personnel.
- Number of new customers: A sales performance measurement in which the number of new customers is tracked; the number of new customers metric is a tool for measuring the progress of field sales personnel.
- Call answering time: A sales performance measurement in which the length of time to answer telephone calls is tracked since lengthy waits for calls to be answered create a bad first impression with potential customers.
- Handling of complaints: A sales performance measurement in which the number of customer complaints and the handling of those complaints are tracked to gauge and make necessary changes to complaint handling organization, speed, and effectiveness.

MARKETING PERFORMANCE MEASUREMENTS

The following marketing performance measurements:

- Market share: Marketing performance measurement in which the percentage of total sales within its specific market that a company holds in opposition to its competitors is calculated and tracked over time
- Lost business analysis: A marketing performance measurement in which decreased sales or unrealized anticipated sales increases are studied to understand the cause and develop solutions
- Promotions and advertising to plan: A marketing performance measurement in which the actual promotions and advertising and their results are tracked and compared to the planned promotions and advertising and their expected results to identify and resolve discrepancies

FLEXIBILITY MEASUREMENTS

Flexibility measurements are performance measurements gauging a company's level of flexibility; flexibility is optimized by minimizing the length of time required to execute tasks so that resources can be committed to tasks later

Volume flexibility is the extent to which a company can vary its production volume in order to meet demand; volume flexibility is achieved through low break-even points, usually in production environments utilizing small, simple, multi-purpose equipment operated by cross-trained personnel so volume can be adjusted profitably in small increments rather than in large, single-process, high-volume environments in which large volumes are typically necessary to reach the break-even point

Product mix flexibility is the extent to which a company can vary its manufacturing product mix in order to meet demand; product mix flexibility requires the ability to change from production of one item to another, usually through quick setup times

VOLUME FLEXIBILITY MEASUREMENTS

Includes vendor lead times, capacity utilization, flexibility of personnel, supplier quality, and the level of purchased inventory. Shorter vendor lead times, lower utilization of capacity, a more flexible and multi-skilled workforce, a higher level of raw materials and component inventory on parts whose purchase lead time is long, and higher supplier quality, especially supplier certification, all increase volume flexibility by decreasing the amount of time required for production. Shorter production times delay the commitment of resources to and shorten the time span necessary for manufacturing tasks required for timely completion.

PRODUCT MIX FLEXIBILITY MEASUREMENTS

Includes order entry time, schedule change time, machine changeover time, manufacturing cycle times, new product introduction time, and flexibility of personnel. Decreasing the lengths of time required to change from manufacturing one item to another increases product mix flexibility. The times required to enter product orders into the system and thus drive manufacturing changes, to change and implement those changes in the manufacturing schedule, and to perform machine changeovers to manufacture different products should all be minimized. The manufacturing cycle times for items produced and the time required for introduction of new products should also be minimized to increase product mix flexibility. Finally, multi-skilled, flexible workers increase product flexibility.

ORDER WINNING STRATEGY

ROLE OF TOP MANAGEMENT

Order winning strategy is the key issue in planning for competitiveness. Primary order winning strategies are price quality, delivery speed, delivery reliability, and flexibility. Top management must develop the production plan with due consideration to order winning strategy. When price is the order-winning strategy, the manufacturing output is usually high-volume and low-variety, continuous or possibly line manufacturing environments. Quality works well as an order winner in low-volume manufacturing (job shop or batch manufacturing environments). Delivery speed is a competitive advantage in job shop and batch manufacturing environments, but not necessarily in line and continuous manufacturing since sales are from stock and speed depends only on the distribution network. Similarly, delivery reliability is dependent on internal manufacturing in job shop environments, but deliveries are made from stock in other environments. In job shop or batch manufacturing environments, flexibility is achieved through capacity underutilization. In line and continuous manufacturing, flexibility can be achieved through volume and variety changes within product families.

EFFECT ON MASTER SCHEDULE

Operations management must develop the master schedule from the production plan with due consideration to order winning strategy. Price as an order-winning strategy usually occurs in high-volume, low-variety manufacturing like job shop or possibly batch manufacture, resulting in long manufacturing runs and stable master schedules. Quality as an order winner typically does not significantly affect the master schedule. When delivery speed or delivery reliability is the order winner, lead time is essential and the master schedule must be practical and well managed. Flexibility as an order winner requires available capacity, through underutilization, and a master schedule that can handle changes in product volume and variety.

EFFECTS ON MATERIAL REQUIREMENTS PLANNING

Operations management must plan material requirements from the master schedule with due consideration to order winning strategy. Price as an order-winning strategy usually occurs in high-volume, low-variety manufacturing, where material requirements planning (MRP) is typically more straightforward due to simpler bills of material. Quality as an order winner typically does not significantly affect MRP. Delivery speed and reliability as order winners rely on the accuracy of lead time data used in MRP, and any changes or priority orders are handled through the MRP rescheduling system. Delivery reliability is difficult in low-volume, high-variety businesses, but can be attained through careful material planning and execution. Flexibility is also difficult in low-volume, high-variety businesses, but can be achieved through ongoing rebalancing and rescheduling of priorities and careful execution.

EFFECT ON OPERATIONS MANAGEMENT EXECUTION

Price is typically an order winner in high-volume, low-variety manufacturing environments like continuous manufacturing, where continued success in maintaining low prices depends on low-cost materials, uninterrupted material flow into production, and continuous operation without stoppage. Quality as on order winner usually occurs in low-volume, high-variety manufacturing environments and has little effect on production execution. Delivery speed as an order winner requires excellent planning and execution in production, and finished goods inventory and underutilized capacity also help. Delivery reliability as an order winner depends on extra inventory and good production management and execution in high-volume, low-variety environments. Delivery reliability is harder to maintain as an order winner in low-volume, high-variety environments, but it can be done through underutilization of capacity and close monitoring of the production schedule. Flexibility as an order winner requires readily available materials for production, availability of capacity, and flexible personnel.

Quick Market Response and JIT

In the current manufacturing and marketing environments, quick market response is essential. Responding quickly to market changes means new products as well as changes to existing products. The just-in-time (JIT) manufacturing framework provides quick market response. Because of the low inventories and quick changeovers characteristic of JIT manufacturing, engineering changes can be simple, quick, and cost effective. Once changes have been approved, they can be implemented at the outset of the next manufacturing frozen period. The items produced between the change decision and its implementation in the next frozen period can be easily handled since there is not significant inventory to handle in addition.

Engineering Change Management

The product being manufactured is defined in the bill of material (BOM) for that product. The BOM is a crucial component of the manufacturing process since it provides a blueprint for building the product. The BOM must be controlled so that unauthorized changes are not made, and there must be an organized method for making authorized changes. Changes to the BOM must be quickly and effectively authorized and implemented to maintain quick market response. A prerequisite for quick market response and good engineering change control is the minimization of changes. A great number of changes is hard to manage quickly and effectively. A good participative design process, ensuring simple, holistic design and sufficient planning, minimizes engineering changes. Engineering changes should reflect market changes, rather than past mistakes.

Engineering Change Control

The process of controlling engineering changes involves an engineering change control board, with representatives from all company departments, including design, industrial engineering, materials, production, quality, finance, and marketing. The departmental representatives must be high-level since they can authorize product changes and implementation of those changes. A dedicated coordinator administrates the whole process. Any department or individual desiring a product change submits a change request with supporting documentation to the coordinator, who then distributes it to the departmental representatives on the change control board. The departmental representatives examine the proposed changes for impact on their individual departments, and meet together to discuss and approve or reject the changes. The coordinator notifies the requestor of the change's acceptance or rejection, and then implements the change appropriately if accepted. It is important that access to actual bills of material is restricted to the change coordinator and their supervisor, so temporary and/or unauthorized changes cannot be made.

Prerequisites for Change

The primary prerequisite for successfully bringing change to a company is a thorough understanding of the company environment. The relational climate, company culture, leadership attitudes, union attitudes, local values, regional economics, and the age, education level, and experience of workers are all aspects of the company's environment which must be understood so that change can be implemented appropriately to ensure success. The values, behavior patterns, and change readiness at work in the company environment must all be considered. Successful change requires total quality management (TQM) values and behavior patterns based on respect for and empowerment of individual employees. If these or change readiness are absent, preliminary general work with regard to these issues must be undertaken so that change can come successfully.

Change Management

Change management begins with identification of the need for change and encompasses everything through the final execution. Both business and people issues are central to change. A company's order winning strategy and production environment are the foundational motivations for change within the company. Changes are made to better support the company strategy and better execute the production environment needed for the company to be competitive. Commitment to the change from both management and personnel is necessary for success. People typically do not want to change. Some steps for gaining employee agreement to and involvement in the change include early announcement of the change so they are not taken by surprise, introduction of the change in incremental stages that are easier to digest, involvement of all staff in the change execution discussions and process, and thorough staff training relating to the change. Implementing change requires time, money, and work, but companies unwilling to change or that wait too long to change will not succeed.

Phases of Change

The first phase of change is identification of the project to be undertaken. The problem to be solved or improvement to be made is earmarked and a solution is identified. The second phase of change is planning. The project is broken down into the steps necessary for completion, which are mapped out according to a timeline. The third phase of change is the action phase. The action phase involves further breakdown of steps required into their components and the development of and agreement on new operating procedures. The fourth phase is implementation, in which the actual changes are executed and the new replaces the old. The fifth phase of change is reorganization, in which problems are addressed and the change is solidified in the company and its operations. The sixth phase is systemization, when any additional changes related to or required by the project are carried out to maximize improvement. Finally, the seventh phase is project closure or ending the change process, after which business proceeds as usual.

Change Planning

For successful change planning, it is necessary for management to provide ongoing, visible support for the project from start to finish. It is also necessary that all staff at every level be motivated to successfully complete the project. This is called buy-in, which is accomplished by all staff seeing that the project is beneficial to them personally and the company as a whole. This is especially important in the case of end users if the project is to be successful. Education and training for the steering committee, the project team, and the end users is also essential so that they will not only be motivated for successful completion but also understand the foundational concepts behind and the principles of the change. Finally, project team members and task team members must accept ownership of the project through responsibility and accountability.

Change Closure

For successful change closure, it is necessary to analyze the project goals and substantiate that they have actually been met. The project was successful only if the goals were successfully met. Beyond that, the closeout support necessary is the assurance of continued project success through auditing and training. Periodic audits, typically yearly, serve the purpose of checking up on the process to verify that the change is still being handled as intended so that there is no breakdown of benefits reaped. Furthermore, sufficient training material must be put in place so that new staff can undertake project-related roles effectively without compromising the project's effectiveness.

Change Implementation

In addition to aligning resources to fulfill the strategic plan and structuring operations to support the plan, strategic management of resources requires successfully implementing change. Change includes the small, steady steps of continuous improvement as well as major overhauls. Changes are implemented in many ways within the different operational management systems, but a system must be in place. Success in the competitive market requires an atmosphere of change. Continuous examination and resulting change enable a company to reach its objectives on an ongoing basis. Change implementation includes project management, organizational performance measurement, and change management.

For successful change implementation, it is necessary for the project plan to be continually revisited and modified to reflect the actual progress and ongoing changes, so that everyone can be on track and working toward the goal appropriately in light of the current situation. Besides maintaining an up-to-date project plan, the focus of implementation is the end users. The project team must involve the end users as much as possible in order to motivate them for successful implementation and to obtain their input. Two specific and practical methods of involvement for end users are the development of specifications so that the ultimate change will be functional for them, and thorough education in the mechanics of using the end product, which is different from the planning stage's education in the concepts and principles driving the change.

Role of Education and Training in Successful Change Implementation

Education is the tool used for motivating the people toward the change and enabling them to achieve it successfully. This is important because the people are the chief change agents. Education can take the form of readings, seminars, visits, hands-on training, and, at best, a combination of these. The education should be timed so that workers gain understanding as they need it for practical use. Before that is too soon. Education consists of both attitude change and information transfer. For attitude change, it is necessary that management visibly supports the change and that education is a long-term process. Successful transfer of information requires repetition as well as hands-on training for the transition from theory to practice.

How Education and Training Apply to the Different Levels of Employees in Change Implementation

Senior management needs a thorough understanding of the motivation for the change and the impact it will have throughout the company so that they can assist as necessary and show clear and appropriate care and concern for the project. The actual project team, usually department managers, must be educated as widely as senior management, but much more deeply since they actually execute the change. Project task team members, typically mid-management and staff, require a general understanding of the change itself and a thorough understanding of the change as it applies to them and their own area of responsibility. Their depth of knowledge is more specific to their responsibility than is the case with project team members. Lastly, the actual manufacturing workers affected by the change must accept the change and understand practically how to use the new methods. Their willingness is the foundation for success.

Preparing Employees for Change

Successful change implementation requires that the employees cooperate with the change and are capable of making the change. A prerequisite to employee cooperation is job security, which includes feelings of comfort, safety, competence, and appreciation from management and colleagues for the job done. The three steps of preparing employees for change are change-related communication, education, and reward. These steps are especially necessary in competitive and profitable manufacturing organizations since the need for change may not be as obvious to the workers. Change communication involves informing the workforce of the anticipated change, its associated concepts, and the reasons behind the change. This communication helps the employees understand the change. Change education involves equipping the workers for the change so that they feel and are capable of the transition and execution. Change reward involves motivating the workers toward the change by showing them what they individually and the company as a whole stand to gain.

Role of Communication

The communication required in order to prepare employees for change includes an assessment of the current situation and its problems necessitating the change as well as the proposed solution to be implemented in response. Details of the proposed solution that constitutes the change, such as scheduling, leadership, and employee involvement and responsibility, should be included in the communication. When there is not open communication about the change, workers make assumptions that lead to fear, unwillingness, and uncooperativeness. Overcoming these wrong assumptions is more difficult than communicating openly from the beginning.

Job Security

The primary fear workers have regarding change is that layoffs will occur as a result of the change. The traditionally adversarial relationship between employees and/or unions and management only serves to feed this fear. Communication is necessary in order to reinforce job security and for leadership to express commitment to the employees. In the current manufacturing environment, management and unions should share the goal of meeting employee needs. Since workers do not tend to believe that management is committed to them and their needs, management effort, patience, consistency, and follow-through are necessary to build a relationship of mutual trust. Management commitment to employees can be carried out by committing to keep all employees regardless of the change. If the change reduces the number of workers needed, management can wait for normal attrition to reduce the workforce to the desired number, or extra workers can be utilized in new expansion projects. Workers must realize and accept that their responsibilities will change for the good of the company.

Job Opportunities

A company can seek to fill a vacancy internally or externally. The chosen candidate should have the skills and experience necessary to successfully perform the job. External candidates may have performed a similar job previously, but still must learn the company culture and politics as well as the product line. Internal candidates may not have performed a similar job previously, but are already well versed in the company culture, politics, and products. Additionally, internal candidates have displayed faithful service and commitment to the company, and their track record is known. Promoting from within contributes to the overall job security atmosphere within a firm. The workers see that management is committed to them and believe in them, and they have hope for their own futures within the company. Hope for the future is the primary ingredient of security.

Role of Education

The education portion of preparing workers for change involves equipping the workers to practically handle the change. It is instilling the capability for change within the workers in addition to the willingness for change instilled through communication. Through education, the unknown and even mysterious nature of the change is replaced with practical understanding and skills. This is necessary since changes typically entail increased complexity, or advancement. The new way can seem overwhelming in comparison to the old way. Change education begins with assessment of needs and training in the general principles involved. From there, a matrix is developed detailing the educational needs of all workers to attain the expertise necessary for successful implementation. Insufficient education may be the most common cause of implementation failure. Its importance is often underestimated.

Courses and Training

The following as they relate to change education:

- Executive overview course: Principle-based training for upper level management enabling them to understand the general concepts and make informed decisions (typically two days in length)
- Five-day course: Practical and detailed training along with principle-based education for project team members (typically five days in length)
- Software training: External training provided by the software supplier for the project team members so they can understand how the related general principles are applied by in the selected software
- Module training: Internal training developed by the project team to teach the system users to use the selected software within the company's particular context
- Simulation training: Trial runs of the system conducted with actual users for educational purposes
- Specific theoretical education: Individual education required for workers to successfully transition to the new job responsibilities required as a result of the change
- General principles education: Training for any and all workers on the general principles underlying the change and the resulting new system

Management Levels

Extensive management hierarchies do not add value to products. In fact, they are costly and time-consuming as well as non-value adding. Reducing the levels of management through delegating responsibility to workers and lower-level leaders is the much-improved current trend. That way, decisions are made in the environment and by the people who are most impacted. Enabling workers and their direct supervisors to make their own decisions reduces management levels and broadens responsibility at each level, resulting in greater flexibility, cross training, and job rotation; improved communication and team building; and easier implementation of just-in-time (JIT) manufacturing principles.

Management by Walking Around

"Management by walking around" refers to the practice on the part of all levels of management of spending time in the factory with the supervisors, workers, and other personnel with the goal of enhancing worker performance through communication. This communication enhances worker performance by meeting the psychological needs of the workers. The communication can include business matters, personal matters, manufacturing problems, expression of commitment and feedback in both directions (from workers to management and from management to workers), and more. From this communication management can gain a better understanding of problems and their causes, discuss potential improvements with those most affected, better evaluate the staff's personal development progress and needs, and come to a clearer understanding of worker culture. "Management by walking around" can be difficult to implement since traditionally managers command rather than communicate and are viewed by workers as adversaries rather than allies.

Hierarchical and Horizontal Management

The hierarchical managements structure is the old framework in which the company is run by a chief officer, to whom departmental executives report, to whom departmental managers report, and so on through many levels, finally reaching the actual operators who report to their supervisors. At each level, responsibility is with the leader, who either makes the decisions or receives them from higher up and requires the people to follow and/or execute them. The horizontal management structure is the new framework in which top management plans for the future and sets organizational policies and priorities, middle management is much reduced and bears broader responsibilities to coordinate operations and serve as knowledge bases and guides to the workers, who are actually responsible for day-to-day operations and associated decision-making. In this setup the workers are multi-skilled and generally more knowledgeable and educated and thus capable of taking responsibility and making decisions.

Employee Empowerment

Employees who are empowered tend to be more efficient and productive in the workplace. Techniques for building employee empowerment include: 1) Encouragement. Encouraging employees through helpful suggestions can empower employees by helping them understand exactly what is expected of them, which allows them to do their jobs with more confidence. 2) Positive reinforcement. Providing positive feedback and praise is another way to empower employees, as people tend to work better when they feel their efforts are being appreciated. 3) Rewards. Tangible thanks or rewards for meeting production goals are a good technique to empower employees and add increased motivation in the workforce. 4) Offer leadership opportunities. Offering employees leadership opportunities, such as supervising a group or heading a project, offers an increased sense of responsibility, leading to empowerment.

Span of Control

In the past, companies have been divided into large, specialized departments that oversaw one aspect of the operation for the entire business, such as materials or technical support. The departments were isolated and functioned separately. Today, the idea of business units is replacing the operating departments. A small group of people is responsible for one segment of the business, such as a particular product. Business units are like small factories within the organization. They are smaller than operational departments, but less specialized and responsible for a wider range of responsibilities. They handle all of the operations necessary for their product or area of responsibility. Business units create feelings of ownership and involvement among their staff and management as they see one product through all stages. The workers are no longer isolated contributors to a monolithic system without visible results. Successful business units provide greater job satisfaction and business success.

Specialization and Job Rotation

Within the horizontal management structure, there is a lower level of specialization and a higher level of job rotation than in the traditional, hierarchical structure.

Both managers and workers must be more flexible and less specialized so that they are capable of fulfilling their horizontal roles. Some specialization will always be necessary, especially for technical issues and expertise, but implementation of horizontal practices such as quality circles requires a broad, general outlook on the part of managers and workers.

Both managers and workers can develop better as well-rounded employees who understand the overall organization, its objectives, and how the different departments and functions work together through job rotation. This enables them to perform better within their horizontal roles through better communication, increased motivation, and greater understanding of the system and other roles within the system.

Job Enlargement and Enrichment

Job enlargement is a job design concept related particularly to production jobs. It is the enlargement or broadening of the job in question through raising the number of activities executed with the goal of higher job satisfaction for the worker. Additional tasks assumed can include maintenance for the equipment used, quality inspections for the products produced, and operation of additional manufacturing equipment. Job enlargement is based on flexibility rather than the specialization necessary for continuous flow manufacturing. The worker is a valuable, multi-skilled team member rather than a number in the system endlessly repeating the same mindless task. Job enrichment is job enlargement with corresponding growth in the responsibility for or control over the activities executed.

Rewards

The benefits of successful change implementation should be evident. The primary reward for the change process for management and workers alike is the obvious improvement brought about by the change. The whole company has improved, and with it the workers. In addition, worker job security grows as the company's competitiveness and profitability grow. For some workers, the opportunities for new jobs and promotions have been realized. For all workers, the new skills learned and contributions made to the company at large can produce feelings of competence and value-added to the company.

Leadership Style

The leadership style of change management presupposes that the role of leaders is to communicate the vision for the future to the workers so that the workers in turn can perform independently and cooperatively to realize that vision. The workers are involved in necessary changes from the beginning to the end, and are an essential part of change management and organization. The leadership style of change management is in direct opposition to the dictatorial management style, in which the workers simply perform as directed without understanding or motivation. The leadership management style requires management to lead by example rather than by commands, to communicate openly and honestly and expect and allow workers to do the same, and to foster innovation, creativity, and improvement. The leadership management style requires involvement, problem solving, and decision making on the part of workers.

Supervision vs. Coaching

In the old-fashioned discipline approach, supervisors used fear and intimidation tactics to compel the workers to perform as required. In the current coaching or guidance approach, the supervisor is responsible for developing the employee into the best that they can be. Under the guidance approach, workers are no longer automations performing as dictated as they were in the discipline approach. They are free agents expected to take initiative to meet company goals and improve processes and products. The foundational practices for success in the guidance approach to employee supervision are education and training, performance measurement, and work procedures.

Scope of Education, Metrics, and Procedures in Structuring Supervision According to the Coaching or Guidance Approach

Employee education should include augmentation of shortcomings in basic education, establishment of operator skills, and instruction in problem solving and supervision, all with the purpose of enabling employees to contribute meaningfully to company goals and improvements. Performance measurements should be in place for supervisors and workers. Supervisors are judged based on their ability to motivate workers, their team-building skills, and employee performance, particularly as related to increasing job flexibility. Workers are judged based on acquisition of skills, team participation, and willingness to shoulder responsibility. Standardized work procedures are necessary for consistent and repeatable quality regardless of the worker executing the task(s). Workers should be involved in setting the procedures and standards. Mistake proofing mechanisms are a valuable tool in setting procedures and standards.

Labor Grades

Grading labor is the practice of distinguishing different types of workers according to their level or type of skill. The labor grade is the classification assigned to an employee. In horizontal management structures, it is desirable to minimize the number of labor grades by widening the scope of each grade. This allows for flatter management structure since widening the scope of each grade and decreasing the number of grades means fewer management levels. The workers and the decision makers are then closer and can communicate better. Minimizing labor grades through broadening their scope also allows workers to use more of their skills and strengths for the good of the company, instead of restricting their contribution, as is the case in narrow grades. Since labor grades have traditionally provided employees with feelings of job security, this need must be met in other ways to implement the change without employee resistance. Financial rewards, either one-time payments or increased wages, can be used to encourage acquisition of new skills.

Ongoing Education and Training

Ongoing education and training encourage workforce involvement simply because they equip the workers to contribute meaningfully in the workplace. Without ability to contribute, employees will shy away from doing so or will contribute ineffectively. Education and training include external and internal offerings in basic skills, specialized and/or job-related skills, and management skills. Specialized and job-related knowledge includes the latest technological developments, information on the implementation and function of new systems, and ongoing systems training. Job rotation and cross-functional training are also training and education, with the goals of higher flexibility and broader organizational understanding. Education and training benefit both the individual workers and the company as a whole.

Internal and External Education

Internal education refers to courses and other training provided by a company's own personnel and resources, while external education refers to courses and other training provided by outside experts. Both types of training are intended to benefit the workers individually and the company as a whole. Internal education typically includes instruction in basic work skills, management skills, necessary job qualifications, and general educational improvement. Company-specific policies, procedures, and applications are handled internally. External education usually involves instruction related to public qualifications, educational improvement, specialized topics, and developmental and technological seminars and courses.

Basic education is academic instruction in general educational skills, beginning with things that should have been acquired in school like reading, writing, and basic math, progressing all the way to knowledge required for external public certifications and qualifications

Technical education is hands-on instruction in a specific discipline or skill set, especially as related to a particular trade or job function, and the knowledge and theory underlying the skill, discipline, or job function

Behavioral education is non-technical and non-academic instruction geared towards behavior and attitude; some examples of behavioral education include management skills, negotiation skills, facilitation skills, and people skills

Workforce Involvement

The bottom line benefit of workforce involvement is continuous improvement. A workforce that is motivated and fully engaged by the company strategy and goals at every level will constantly improve the company. Successful workforce involvement yields a workforce that is educated and equipped to contribute meaningfully to the company's progress and that is actively involved in running the company day-to-day, and management that relates directly to the workforce without hiding behind hierarchical structure and is not distracted by day-to-day "emergencies." Workforce involvement produces ongoing change, exactly what is needed for continuous improvement.

Continuous and Process Improvement

Continuous improvement is the ongoing process of eliminating waste and solving problems in the production process. Waste is anything that is unnecessary in the production process, and solving problems entails identifying and eliminating the root causes, not simply coping. Both managers and workers are involved, and improvements tend to be small rather than large. Continuous improvement is also referred to as continuous process improvement (CPI) and kaizen, the Japanese term for improvement.

Process improvement can be accomplished in two ways, either by better executing and solving problems within the existing process or by changing the process itself. The first approach lends itself to small, ongoing changes while the second lends itself to major, one-time changes. The biggest obstacle to continuous and/or process improvement is resistance to change. An atmosphere of ongoing improvement must be purposefully created so that employees will continually make suggestions.

Configuring and Integrating Operations

For manufacturing operations to support the strategic plan, they must be configured and integrated appropriately. How the operational control processes interact with other business choices, the volume and variety of products manufactured by the company, the company's competitive position, and the company's strategy must all be considered simultaneously. Prerequisite to this task is a complete understanding of the company's current operations in relation to the actual demand and anticipated future demand, as well as other factors like order-winning strategy, expected changes, and need for flexibility. This is called product profiling. The actual steps required to configure and integrate operations to support the strategic plan are implementing the strategic plan, managing the company's supply chain in line with the strategic plan, and implementing appropriate design and development and cost management processes.

Implementing Plan in Operations

The process of implementing the strategic plan in operations encompasses structuring the operations management system with regard to its interactions with other business functions, like marketing and sales, engineering and design, logistics, finance and accounting, and human resources. In addition, the operations management system must be configured according to the company's volume-variety mix at all levels, including top management planning, operations management planning, and operations management execution. Operations must also support company competitiveness through processes and structural combinations that support the company's order winning strategy. All of these steps must be performed with the company's strategic plan as the ultimate goal.

CPIM Practice Test

Want to take this practice test in an online interactive format?
Check out the online resources page, which includes interactive practice questions and much more: **mometrix.com/resources719/cpimsmr**

1. The statement that best describes the characteristics of a market driven manufacturer is:

a. A market driven manufacturer decides what to make through market and consumer research and sales analysis
b. A market driven manufacturer chooses to make a popular product better than competitors
c. A market driven manufacturer contracts outside, independent companies to determine what should be manufactured
d. A market driven manufacturer makes whatever it wants to make

2. Three components of a successful product manufacturing business strategy are:

a. Financial operations, engineering, and marketing
b. Cell design, materials, and external supply sources
c. Manufacturing operations, inventory, and external supply sources
d. Price leadership, product differentiation, and customer focus

3. A customer has the choice of several smart phones (and manufacturers) that meet functional requirements, but chooses the iPhone. From this selection one may say that:

a. The iPhone is an order qualifier
b. The iPhone is an order winner
c. The iPhone is both an order qualifier and an order winner
d. The iPhone is neither an order qualifier nor an order winner

4. A certain product may be the reason a company becomes an order winner but sometimes it is the company itself. The statement that best explains the latter is:

a. Distinctive competencies refer to a company's unique strengths that attract customers
b. Distinctive competencies refer to a company's image as an order qualifier
c. Distinctive competencies refers to a company's ability to deliver differentiated, lower-cost products
d. Distinctive competencies refers to novel marketing and product engineering strategies

5. The statement that best explains why an order qualifier is not always an order winner is:

a. Customers are impulsive and don't pay attention to quality considerations
b. Customers always respond to price advantages rather than order qualification
c. Customers do not always recognize quality or may confuse packaging with real quality
d. Customers are always seeking something different so they are more interested in product differentiation than quality

6. One of the four approaches to developing an operations strategy is termed the overview approach. The overview approach can be defined as being:

a. Focused upon the interrelationship between operational functions
b. Focused upon primary operational factors like resources, capacity, and technology used in integrating the manufacturing process
c. Focused upon determining the original causes of capacity trade-offs and eliminating them
d. Setting an order for the four competing priorities and completes action sequentially

7. One of the four approaches to developing an operations strategy is termed the reductionist approach. The reductionist approach can be defined as being:

a. Focused upon the interrelationship between operational functions
b. Focused upon primary operational factors like resources, capacity, and technology used in integrating the manufacturing process
c. Focused upon determining the original causes of capacity trade-offs and eliminating them
d. Setting an order for the four competing priorities and completes action sequentially

8. One of the four approaches to developing an operations strategy is termed the sequential approach. The sequential approach can be defined as being:

a. Focused upon the interrelationship between operational functions
b. Focused upon primary operational factors like resources, capacity, and technology used in integrating the manufacturing process
c. Focused upon determining the original causes of capacity trade-offs and eliminating them
d. Setting an order for the four competing priorities and completes action sequentially

9. One of the four approaches to developing an operations strategy is termed the tradeoff approach. The tradeoff approach can be defined as being:

a. Focused upon the interrelationship between operational functions
b. Focused upon primary operational factors like resources, capacity, and technology used in integrating the manufacturing process
c. Focused upon determining the original causes of capacity trade-offs and eliminating them
d. Setting an order for the four competing priorities and completes action sequentially

10. A type of manufacturing designed to occur 24 hours a day and 7 days per week is called:

a. Perpetual motion manufacturing
b. Line manufacturing
c. Continuous manufacturing
d. Four-walled batch manufacturing

11. The statement that best explains why product design and product image can result in order winners is:

a. Product design determines cost of manufacture; product image determines consumer buying habits
b. Creating product image adds to the expense of manufacture, but product design can make up for shortfalls in demand
c. Product design is founded on customer needs and products must be timely delivered; order winning follows upon a positive perception of products in the marketplace
d. All of the above

12. The volumes and range of products produced are company structural decisions which must be made, and once made, are difficult to reverse. Other structural decisions involved in the strategic resource management include:

a. Plant location and size, manufacturing methods, and work cell design
b. Capital requirements and financing
c. Marketing and sales strategies
d. All of the above

13. Which of the five steps of the manufacturing transformation process pertains to the production of goods that are not finished products themselves but rather are used to build other products?

a. Assembly distribution
b. Fabrication of parts
c. Primary resource creation
d. Assembly

14. Which of the five steps of the transformation process involves the acquisition and collection of raw materials?

a. Assembly distribution
b. Fabrication of parts
c. Primary resource creation
d. Assembly

15. Which of the five steps of the transformation process entails customer interactions such as sales and product delivery transactions?

a. Material distribution
b. Service and delivery
c. Primary resource creation
d. Sales and marketing

16. Preproduct development is one of the six phases of a product life cycle. Preproduct development may be defined as:

a. The process of establishing product specifications and forecasting and filling early demand for the product
b. The process of accumulating and shipping raw materials needed for manufacture
c. The process of testing and product introduction
d. General research that informs the decision-making process for what product(s) to pursue

17. The steady-state phase of the six-stage product life cycle chain refers to:

a. A period in the manufacturing process in which production volumes are fixed and unchanging
b. A period in the manufacturing process in which product demand is rising at a steady pace
c. A period in the manufacturing process in which manufacturing demand and customer orders are stable and predictable
d. A period in the manufacturing process in which product demand is diminishing at a steady pace

18. Among the reasons for the phase-out stage of product life cycle are:

a. Product obsolesence, lack of availability of raw materials or components, increased competition
b. Decreased demand, company choice of a replacement product, or external forces
c. Additional costs associated with government regulation, economic downturns, higher interest rates
d. All of the above

19. After research, testing, design, and introduction of a new product, the next phase of the product life cycle is:

a. Product development
b. Steady state
c. Phase out
d. Rapid growth

20. The disadvantage of using leading demand indicators as the basis for an increase in manufacturing volume is:

a. That leading demand figures are imaginary, with no basis in actual manufacturing
b. That leading demand is an actual figure that does not account for spikes in demand
c. That leading demand is a forecast figure and actual demand may vary too much
d. That leading demand is a method of launching incremental volume increases

21. Using lagging demand indicators to determine production output volume carries the risk of:

a. Producing an oversupply of finished product when lagging demand reflects declining demand
b. Producing an oversupply of finished products when external forces increase market demand
c. Losing customers when the factory cannot meet actual demand
d. Causing excessive inventory buildup when demand increases

22. The best definition of the tracking/chasing demand method of setting capacity is:

a. A decision to increase capacity based on demand forecasting alone
b. A decision to increase manufacturing capacity based on actual demand and incremental capacity increases
c. A decision to increase capacity based on tracking actual sales
d. Capacity decisions are set by market research trends

23. Assuming that factory equipment and machinery are sufficient to meet capacity demands, the quickest way to address output capacity shortages is:

a. Hiring of additional workers to supplement the existing workforce
b. Leaner inventories and kanban
c. Overtime and subcontracting
d. Expanding the facility by additional building

24. Viable factory location options for a new manufacturing planner DO NOT always include:

a. Building factories in cities where largest markets lie
b. Storing goods in warehouses close to large metropolitan market areas
c. Building factories near to major transportation arteries
d. Building factories near large markets combined with warehouse storage in other areas

25. Factors that come into play in the distribution planning for a new manufacturing location are:

a. Competitor locations, competitor pricing, number of competitors
b. Warehousing, storage, handling costs
c. Nearness to large markets, major transportation arteries, and factory location
d. Availability of financing, availability of labor, availability of suppliers

26. Using auto manufacturing as an example of inventory and supply problems, common problems in the supply chain include all of the following EXCEPT:

a. A global supply chain
b. Dealer inventory
c. Nearness to transportation arteries
d. Competition from foreign auto makers

27. Which of the following statements is NOT TRUE?

a. Proximity to customer market diminishes lead times and transportation costs while increasing responsiveness
b. Proximity to suppliers is especially important in the delivery of cumbersome materials because of higher costs associated with them
c. Manufacturing plants should ideally be located near customer markets and suppliers
d. Central warehousing is as important as factory location in an efficient distribution network

28. The impact of wages on factory location is best described by which of the following statements?

a. The availability of a cheap unskilled labor force always leads to higher profitability
b. The key factor regarding worker wages is the skill level involved in relation to the wage scale
c. Wages can always be negotiated in a manner that is favorable to the manufacturing environment
d. Wages are never a factor in choosing factory location

29. The impact of tax rates on factory location is best described by which of the following statements?

a. State, local, and corporate tax rates are a primary concern in choosing the location of a manufacturing facility
b. State, local, and corporate tax rates are high everywhere you go so it is not as important as other factors in choosing factory location
c. State, local, and corporate taxation diminish in importance as a basis for factory location choice during an economic downturn where profits are marginal
d. State, local, and corporate taxation are strictly political matters and not practical ones

30. The impact of building and building operation costs on factory location is best described by which of the following statements?

a. Costs are higher in some locations than in others, but this has no impact on the bottom line
b. Distribution costs are always higher than building and operating costs in a particular environment, so these costs are of low priority
c. Costs are higher in some locations and lower in others, but these costs have to be balanced against cost of transportation and proximity to markets
d. All of the above

31. If the cost of taxes, labor, and real estate near major consumer markets were to be graphically represented, the graph would show:

a. Tax rates, labor wages, and building and operation costs tend to decrease as distance from large major markets increases
b. Tax rates, labor wages, and building and operation costs tend to increase as distance from large major markets increases
c. Tax rates, labor wages, and building and operation costs tend to differ only marginally as distance from large major markets increases
d. Tax rates, labor wages, and building and operation costs tend to be negligible so long as the large consumer markets are in the United States

32. The disadvantage of locating a factory far away from established industrial centers is that:

a. The factory may be too far away from major transportation arteries
b. The factory may be too far away from customer markets
c. Utilities may not be available in sufficient capacity to meet manufacturing goals
d. Utilities may be too costly to meet the needs of planned manufacture

33. Define backward integration as it applies to manufacturing and describe at least one risk.

a. Backward integration means that the factory produces needed supply internally rather than buying it from suppliers; it carries quality and cost risk
b. Backward integration means that the factory cuts out the middle man; it carries the risk of increased costs
c. Backward integration means that a company does its own retailing and distribution; it carries an increased risk of failure because the company may not be efficient at these things
d. Backward integration means that consumer orders are received before manufacturing begins; it carries the risk of being unable to meet spiking demand

34. Forward integration in manufacturing means:

a. Manufacturing product families simultaneously with individual product lines
b. Replacing goods previously purchased with internally supplied goods
c. Information sharing with suppliers
d. Entering into retail sales and product distribution

35. Employee involvement programs can increase manufacturing efficiency, productivity, and profit. Which of the following is NOT an employee involvement tool?

a. Cross-functional problem solving
b. Seniority system
c. Merit award system
d. Quality circles

36. Two of the best methods for involving employees in a team effort to improve manufacturing efficiency are:

a. Education programs and basic skills training
b. Quality circles and cross-functional problem solving
c. Suggestion programs and merit awards
d. Appraisal and reward systems

37. Quality circles have been shown to be an effective way of managing human resources. The fundamental components of a successful quality circle are:

a. Leadership, workers, and structure
b. Skill, ownership, and focus
c. Quality, training, and group identity
d. Size, structure, and group identity

38. A cross-functional problem-solving team should include:

a. Only those departments directly involved in the manufacturing
b. Representatives from all departments and disciplines
c. One top level manager, one midlevel operations manager, and all shop forepersons
d. The materials department, the design department, and quality control

39. Of four common methods of worker compensation, the individual incentivized method is:

a. Fixed rate compensation
b. Profit sharing
c. Skill-based rates
d. Piecework pay

40. AQL (acceptable quality level) is a quality control approach that:

a. Eliminates the need for quality testing
b. Measures the quality of all production output by inspection
c. Structuring operations to meet quality requirements
d. Tests the quality of batch samples

41. How is weighted moving average applied to inventory valuation?

a. Weighted moving average is an inventory valuation method in which the actual value of first-in inventory is averaged with first-out inventory
b. Weighted moving average is an inventory valuation method in which all inventory is valued at an average of the latest price and the first price paid
c. Weighted moving average is an inventory valuation method in which all material and components are valued at their average cost
d. Weighted moving average is an inventory valuation method in which the value of inventory is pegged to average market prices

42. The type of manufacturing environment often determines the type of cost accounting method utilized. ABC or activity based costing is a type of accounting that:

a. Is most suitable to onetime made-to-order large projects like bridges or buildings
b. Attributes costs to manufacturing functions
c. Attributes cost to equipment and work centers utilized
d. Is most suitable to homogeneous, high-volume process environments

43. Technology accounting cost measurement is a system in which overhead costs are attributed to equipment rather than to labor or other categories. The rationale for technology accounting is:

a. Equipment and technology costs are the primary cost drivers in manufacturing
b. Equipment and technology costs have traditionally been ignored in cost accounting
c. Equipment and technology costs were traditionally combined into factory overhead categories
d. Equipment and technology depreciation are significant and cannot be effectively averaged or ignored

44. The most accurate example(s) of indirect costs are:

a. Communications, management activity, and utilities
b. Employee health insurance and worker's compensation payments
c. Product advertising and taxation
d. Management perquisites and profit sharing

45. Select the most accurate definition of standard costing from the choices below.

a. Standard costing is based on actual costs of production, but such costs are apportioned equally among various accounting categories
b. Standard costing is based on theoretical target costs and compared with actual costs with a view to establishing cost stabilization
c. Standard costing is the same as "textbook costing," with the difference that production is tracked and averaged for a specific period of time
d. Standard costing tracks each step in the production process and averages that baseline of data to produce a "standard cost"

46. How are equivalent units of production used to calculate unit costs?

a. WIP is counted on a percentage basis; unit cost is obtained by adding that percentage to the percentage of completely finished products within a given time frame
b. Equivalent units of production is a figure equal to unit cost
c. Unit cost is assigned according to a calibrated scale obtained by averaging standard percentage rates of WIP
d. WIP is assigned a percentage completion and the unit equivalent of production is obtained; the actual total cost of production divided by that equivalent unit to yield unit cost

47. The costing system that would most likely be used for a producer of canned soups is:

a. Process costing system
b. Activity based costing system
c. Standard costing system
d. Project costing system.

48. The chief advantages of the cellular organizational structure in manufacturing is:

a. Shorter queues and move times
b. Shorter lead times
c. Smaller space requirements
d. All of the above

49. A well-known axiom in manufacturing is that quality costs. One of the four chief categories of quality cost is the internal failure cost. Internal failure costs are those that:

a. Result from product defects that appear before the product is sold to the customer
b. Result from product defects that appear after the product is sold to the customer
c. Are incurred as the result of inspection, testing, calibration, and quality audits
d. Are incurred as the result of quality training programs and certification

50. External failure costs are one of the four main categories of failure cost. External failure cost refers to:

a. Costs resulting from product defects that appear before the product is sold to the customer
b. Costs resulting from product defects that appear after the product is sold to the customer
c. Costs resulting from inspection, testing, calibration and quality audits
d. Costs incurred in employer quality training programs and certification

Answer Key and Explanations

1. A: The companies that produce goods to meet demand are said to be marketplace driven. The demand in the marketplace is determined through market research, which includes market analysis, sales analysis, and consumer research. Such research can be conducted by the company itself, its designee, or by independently contracted parties. Market-driven means that research determines product demand and also defines how the product can be better made to obtain market share from competitors.

2. D: because the question is addressed toward business strategy. A successful business strategy is one that supersedes current offerings for product development, manufacture, and consumer sales. In order for a product to succeed, the business strategist seeks advantage in price leadership, product differentiation, and a focus upon the customer. Low product prices, unique or improved products, and responsive customer service are essential to a successful business strategy.

3. C: To correctly answer the question, it helps to know the difference between the terms order qualifier and order winner. The so-called smart phone provides a handy example that demonstrates the meaning of both terms. Several manufacturers make smart phones that meet consumer needs, requirements, and demand, yet the popularity of Apple smart-phones borders on obsession. The ability of several manufacturers to product excellent smart phones means that their products are order qualifiers. The ability of Apple to continuously increase their smart phone market share over competitors means it is both order qualifier and order winner.

4. A: considering that the question asks you to choose the statement that explains how a company (rather than the product) is the basic reason it becomes an order winner. Several companies make reliable cars, according to vehicle rating agencies like J. D. Power et al., but a long recognition of superior quality and customer service may drive a company (like Toyota) to acquire market share beyond the qualities of its products. Consider that auto sales records show that Toyota is an order winner in spite of recent well-publicized events. Another example of a company-driven order winner is Ford, not only because it produces order qualifiers, but because the consumer has certain perceptions of the brand and because the ratings agencies (Consumer Reports and J. D. Powers, for example) have characterized the company in a positive way.

5. C: Like price, quality is often an order qualifier rather than an order winner. Customers cannot always differentiate the quality levels of their competing suppliers. An important distinction to make in considering product quality is the difference between actual quality and perceived quality. Customers may perceive products with packaging that looks cheap or other superficial tags as being poor quality, even though they meet all stated specifications. Both actual and perceived quality must be at acceptable levels for success of the product in the marketplace.

6. B: The four approaches to developing an operations strategy are: overview approach, the trade-off approach, the reductionist approach, and the sequential approach. In the overview approach, the method is to consider the primary operational factors such as available resources; technology currently used capacity for integration, philosophy of quality, and internal company relationships. The approach mentioned in choice "d" is called the sequential approach. Choice "c" refers to the reductionist approach and "a" pertains to the trade-off approach.

7. C: Instead of focusing on and balancing process trade-offs, the reductionist approach concentrates on determining the original causes of trade-offs and easing or eliminating them. The reductionist approach is just one of four main business philosophies in the development of operation strategies. The other three business approaches to strategy are termed the trade-off approach, the sequential approach, and the overview approach. The development of a strategic approach is an important analytical tool which helps management to narrow down the multitude of choices which present themselves in manufacturing.

8. D: The sequential approach to the development of a business strategy involves setting an order of completion for four competing priorities. The next in order of priority is not begun until the earlier priority is completed in full and in detail. The sequential approach is just one of four main business philosophies in the development of operation strategies. The other three business approaches to strategy are termed the trade-off approach, the reductionist approach, and the overview approach. The development of a strategic approach is an important analytical tool that helps management to narrow down the multitude of choices that present themselves in manufacturing.

9. A: In the trade-off approach, management considers the interrelationships between operational functions, such as the relationship between customer service and inventory investment or volume of goods produced and cost of goods produced. One function can act as a limit on another and the trade-off approach can help to alleviate the negative or limiting impact of one process upon another. If the volume of goods produced causes prices to drop below the point where profitability is strained, the adoption of the trade-off approach may be the appropriate remedy.

10. C: Continuous manufacturing is the term for the type of manufacturing that is planned to occur continuously—24 hours per day and 7 days per week. Continuous manufacturing is similar to line manufacturing, but with even more specialized equipment and less variety of goods produced. It is a manufacturing environment in which highly specialized equipment is used to produce one or a very few type(s) of set goods in high volumes at an extremely low cost. Product changes and new products occur rarely.

11. C: Product design begins with customer needs. Through the product design process, these needs are defined as product specifications that drive the design process. The effectiveness and speed with which a company learns, quantifies, designs for, and meets customer needs in the marketplace is crucial. It is an order winner. Meeting customer needs and desires before the competition does provides competitive edge and market share. Image is the perception of the company or product in the marketplace. In some industries, image is of paramount importance. Think of Apple CEO Steve Jobs and the iPhone 4.

12. A: Plant location and size and the functional emplacement of the manufacturing work stations are decisions which, once made, are hard to reverse—at least without great expense and lost profits. Marketing and sales strategies, on the other hand, can be revised and made flexible. Capital investment requirements,too, can be altered and financing structure can evolve to meet changing economic circumstances. Since structural changes like plant size and location are so expensive to reverse, it is of utmost important to consider these choices in meticulous detail.

13. B: The chain of transformations, known also as the transformation process, is the sequence of steps from raw materials to finished goods. The sequence is divided into five specific steps: primary resource creation, fabrication of parts, assembly, distribution, and service and delivery. Fabrication of parts is but one step in the transformation process, a step which refers to production of goods that are not finished products themselves but rather are used to build other products.

14. C: The chain of transformations, or the transformation process, is the sequence of steps from initial inputs to final outputs, from raw materials to finished goods. The sequence is divided into five specific steps: primary resource creation, fabrication of parts, assembly, distribution, and service and delivery. Primary resource creation is the initial attainment of raw materials, such as ore, aluminum, steel or whatever raw materials are needed. Primary resource creation companies are considered nonmanufacturing producers.

15. B: Service and delivery are part of a series of five steps in manufacturing a product from its beginning raw materials state to its completion as a finished product. The sequences involved in the transformation process are divided into five specific steps: primary resource creation, fabrication of parts, assembly, distribution, and service and delivery. Service and delivery entails customer interactions such as sales and product delivery transactions.

16. D: Preproduct development is the first stage in a product life cycle. It involves general marketing research, not directed toward a specific product or family product. The purpose of preproduct development is to determine what products might be profitable and stable to manufacture. There may be a range of products that could be profitably manufactured but it is the preproduct development phase that informs decisions as to what type of product manufacture will be actively pursued.

17. C: The steady state phase in a product life cycle occurs when fluctuations and uncertainty of early manufacturing processes are smoothed out. The volumes of items being produced are consistent and better matched to customer demand; customer demand is similarly predictable, even with regard to seasonal changes and demand spikes. At the steady state phase in the product life cycle, the product is well established as an order winner, accounting for stability and predictability in both manufacturing and sales.

18. D: Product life cycles come to their end for the variety of reasons mentioned in all of the answer options. Manufacturing occurs in a constantly changing environment. As with automakers producing a lesser number of models during economic downturns, so can external factors like supply problems or new competitors entering the market cause the phase out of products at the end of the product life cycle. In other areas, digital electronics makes analog products obsolete and companies must adapt to the changes by halting manufacture of outmoded products.

19. D: After product development processes such as research, testing, design, and the introduction of a new product into the marketplace have occurred, there is (ideally) a phase in the product life cycle termed the rapid growth phase. The rapid growth phase is the fourth stage in the product life cycle, and is marked by rising customer demand. This rapid growth phase is followed by the steady state phase, in which demand is predictible and production is stable, and then the product life cycle ends with the phase out stage, the last step in the process.

20. C: Demand predictions factor into manufacturing before and during operations. Leading demand indicators are based on past manufacturing performance over a period of time sufficient for the prediction method. Leading demand based predictions of future volume requirements may overestimate or underestimate actual demand. The impact of inaccurate predictions is either too much finished product buildup or too little product to meet customer demand. In the latter case, there could be a loss of customers; in the former, the overproduction must be stored and handled, and in some cases, may become obsolete.

21. C: Using lagging demand means that manufacturing volume levels are not projected—rather they are based on actual order demand. This can be a handicap in an expanding market where shortages of finished product could result in lost sales. Lagging demand is used when a company is uncertain of future sales, so capacity increase is postponed until actual demand is established.

There are drawbacks to forecast demand also; the type of method employed to set production volume levels should be addressed during market research.

22. B: In the tracking/chasing demand method, the decision to increase manufacturing capacity is based on actual demand and incremental demand increases. Tracking/chasing demand is a hybridized version of the leading and lagging demand methods. Like lagging demand, the disadvantage of the tracking/chasing method of setting capacity is in the amount of time necessary for capacity increases, although the incremental capacity increases can be implemented more quickly.

23. C: Overtime and subcontracting are the fastest ways to address output limitations that are not the result of machine or equipment capacity. Overtime workers can be applied to additional shifts so that maximum output capacity is reached. Leaner inventories and kanban are desirable but do not in themselves increase output capacity. Hiring of new workers and expansion of the factory facility does expand capacity but these adjustments are lengthy processes and not quick ways to increase output.

24. A: The exclusionary aspect of the question is the viability of a new factory location. Take that to mean cost-effective, since profitability is an absolute necessity for successful manufacturing. It may not be possible to build a new factory in New York, or Los Angeles, or Berlin, where zoning laws and regulations combine with cost to make this the most expensive and difficult choice. More viable options include building factories near large markets or major transportation arteries, combined with warehousing near large city markets.

25. C: The correct answer is "c". Other answer options offer real concerns, but those concerns always exist and must be addressed during the preproduction planning period. Warehousing, storage, and handling costs are fixed costs faced by every business, and competitors face them too. So are problems like availability of financing, labor, supply, pricing, and competition. It is so in distribution planning, but the choices have already been made by competitor firms and that does not diminish the importance of distribution planning for a new manufacturing business.

26. D: The answer option that does not fit with the others is "d." Competitiveness is not a supply or inventory problem of the auto business, though one could make a case that auto makers compete for suppliers. The answer to that problem, however, is increased supplier capacity. More basic problems are a global supply chain in which headlight assemblies may be made in one country and transmissions in another. Supplies must often travel by ocean, rail, and road transportation. Finished product inventory is stored in various locations, including dealer lots.

27. D: Except for answer option "d," all of the statements are accurate. In the ideal situation, a manufacturing concern would be located near both customer markets and suppliers, minimizing transportation costs, cutting lead times, and increasing responsiveness. This is especially advantageous in the movement of cumbersome components or dangerous raw materials. On the other hand, central warehousing can augment a distribution network but incur additional expenses of storage, handling, and transportation. In many cases, central distribution warehouses are not needed at all.

28. B: Wages are an important concern in choosing factory location, though it is by no means the only consideration. The key factor regarding worker wages is the requisite skill level for the type of manufacturing involved. Some types of product manufacturing does not require as high a skill level as other types of manufacturing so it is important to match factory location with the skill level required by the type(s) of product being manufactured.

29. A: State, local, and corporate tax rates are a primary concern in choosing the location of a manufacturing facility. Tax rates and categories vary from state to state and corporate tax rates are a political matter but wise planners take it into consideration when choosing factory locations. In an economic downturn, a business-friendly tax policy is especially sought after because it can make the difference between profitabilty and loss.

30. C: The best answer is "c," because the two factors are interrelated. Prime markets are often located in expensive areas but it may be advantageous to locate where reduced costs of shipping and transportation from cheaper locations may counterbalance the impact of expensive real estate. Being close to large markets may result in profitability in spite of high costs of location, but sometimes the opposite is true. It is essential that both factors be given primary consideration in factory location planning.

31. A: Tax rates, labor wages, and building and operation costs are important considerations in determining factory location. These costs vary with location, and tend to decrease as distance from an industrial center increases. However, local governments in high-unemployment or underdeveloped areas may provide tax incentives to encourage the establishment of business. Tax location incentives and increased transportation costs sometimes makes the more expensive location options viable but some types of manufacturing would benefit from the less expensive costs of being farther from major markets.

32. C: The best answer is "c" because the other potential deficiences can be counterbalanced by other factories. Distance from transportation arteries may be compensated by a lower wage base, for example. Utilities are vital for manufacturing, however, and telephone, power, water, and other systems must be in place and capable of handling the level of demand placed on them by a manufacturing facility. Installing or enhancing utilities are possible to meet manufacturing needs, but the associated costs may be prohibitive.

33. A: When a company chooses backward integration, they are replacing goods they previously purchased with internally supplied goods. Assuming that the company can do as good a job as their former supplier at the decreased production volume, they decrease costs by cutting the supplier's profit margin. Additionally, information sharing can be more open than is the case when the supplier also sells goods to competitors. However, this change does introduce added quality and cost risk.

34. D: In implementing forward integration, a company is entering into distribution and retail sales, both of which vary greatly from manufacturing. Advantages include cutting out middleman profit margins and receiving more direct feedback from end users.There are advantages in both cases, but these advantages hinge on the company's success in accomplishing a challenging task, which is not guaranteed. Another process engaged in by some manufacturers is called backward integration, which refers to a change from reliance on outside suppliers to internal ones.

35. B: The seniority system is not an effective employee involvement tool and is sometimes a disincentive to worker initiative. The remaining answer options are common employee involvement tools that have been effectively used to increase quality, productivity, and worker pride. Common employee involvement tools include: suggestion programs, quality circles, cross-functional problem solving teams, appraisal and reward systems, and education and training. They may be used separately or in combination to encourage workers to take an active, personal interest in the task of serving customers.

36. B: Quality circles and cross-functional problem-solving teams are excellent ways to involve larger numbers of employees in the larger activities and goals of manufacturing. Quality circles are small groups of employees who work together as a team, and additionally spend time (typically one hour per week) meeting together with the purpose of improving their product and/or process. Cross-functional problem solving teams are teams of employees from different departments within a company who combine their expertise to solve a particular problem.

37. A: The best answer is "a," because the primary components of a successful quality circle are leadership, workers, and the structure of the group. Leadership entails involving all levels of leaders, from the direct supervisor of the quality group all the way up to top-level management. Leadership support of the groups is essential, as is the skill of the group supervisor in focusing on the goal and facilitating the meetings. The workers themselves must feel ownership of their process and be willing to identify problems.

38. B: Since problems can be located anywhere in the manufacturing chain, so can solutions be found in all the related functions of the sucessful business enterprise. A cross-functional problem solving team should include the marketing and sales, engineering and design, manufacturing, quality assurance, costing, and materials departments. Involving multiple disciplines simultaneously in the problem solving process optimizes time and cost required to solve problems. Since all departments are involved in preproduction, it is logical to include them in teams assigned to remedy problems that develop in forecasting, production, or other processes.

39. D: While all forms of pay may be seen as an incentive, in that getting paid is always an objective, piecework pay is based on the amount of work produced. Piecework pay may applied to individuals or entire work groups collectively. Other methods of compensation include fixed rates, skills-based rates, and profit sharing. Profit sharing is an incentive tool which encourages workers to support other workers in the achievement of manufacturing objectives, whereas methods like piecework pay are targeted toward individual areas or specific work groups.

40. D: The acceptable quality level (AQL) is a tool for measuring a representative sample from a batch of goods (or the whole batch, if the testing is nondestructive) to determine if the defect percentage of the batch is below required limits. Batches that exceed the AQL may be rejected or, alternatively, sold to customers with an open declaration as to increased likelihood of defect. AQL is a quality control technique used to test the quality of goods after they have been produced. Quality assurance is a different approach that depends on the structuring of operations to achieve quality goals.

41. C: Weighted moving average is an inventory valuation method in which all goods stored are valued at their average cost. The order of release from inventory is irrelevant to value so FIFO and LIFO methodology does not apply. With the weighted moving average recordkeeping is simplified, since individual values are not necessary, and the effect of inflation and deflation on production costs is smoothed out. The weighted moving average is calculated by adding the total cost of new items deposited into inventory to the total cost of current inventory and dividing by the number of new and current inventory items.

42. B: The system(s) of cost accounting employed in a given situation is based on the volume and type of manufacturing process utilized. In most situations, some form of standard or process costing is used, with process costing being reserved for homogenous, high-volume, process environments. Project costing is used for substantial, onetime, made-to-order assignments like bridges or buildings, or activity based costing attributes costs to manufacturing functions and activities and technology accounting bases overhead costs on equipment used.

43. D: The best answer choice is "d," although there is an element of truth in other answers. Technology accounting is a manufacturing costing system in which overhead costs for products are determined by the equipment rather than the labor utilized in production. In situations where it is used, the rationale for technology accounting is that it more effectively quantifies overhead costs associated with equipment and technology depreciation. Technology investiment is significant in some kinds of manufacturing and cannot be effectively averaged, ignored, or fit into traditional categories.

44. A: Answer "a" offers the best examples of indirect costs. Indirect costs are difficult to quantify. In general, indirect costs are an assessment of general work center costs that are not attributable to particular jobs performed or goods produced—such as utilities, communication, and management. A related category of costs is termed nonproductive costs and these consist of costs like employee benefits and unassociated material costs which cannot be attributed to the production process.

45. B: Standard costing is a manufacturing costing system based on predetermined target or theoretical costs for operations and materials. Discrepancies between actual and standard costs are recorded and maintained in a variance account. The advantage of standard costing is cost stabilization so that production management and sell price determination are simplified. Standard costs have traditionally been set on a yearly basis, but are now usually set on a quarterly basis.

46. D: Answer choice "d" expresses the method of calculating unit cost. WIP is assigned a percentage completion, and the unit equivalent of production is obtained; the actual total cost of production divided by that equivalent unit to yield unit cost.

For example, the unit equivalent for 100 units of WIP that is 80% complete is 80. Let's suppose the actual total cost of production is $160. The per item cost is obtained by dividing actual total costs by 80. This yields the per unit or per item cost: $160/80 equivalent units = $2 per item.

47. A: The type of manufacturing generally determines the type of cost accounting system most suitable to production in that type of industry. A corporation such as Intel, which manufactures computer chips, would have to heavily invest in technology on a continuous basis. Owing to the fast changing technological environment, that type of financial outlay (and depreciation) can be rarely captured by conventional accounting methods and so technology accounting is used. A producer of canned soup, on the other hand, has fixed known costs (labor, materials, overhead. which do not vary and so process cost accounting is most suitable.

48. A: The correct answer is "a"; the chief advantage of the cellular organizational structure is shorter lines as work moves from one machine stop to another for finishing. The moving distance is shorter and workers have visual sight of work awaiting process. Cellular organization augments JIT manufacturing, and work is much easier to schedule than in other configurations. Traditional in-line layouts, sometimes termed the functional layout, do just the opposite and machines and processes of identical type are located together. This means the batches of work must move together to the next work station in the routing sequence on the way to completion—increasing lead time.

49. A: Internal failure costs are those that result from product defects that appear before the product is shipped to the customer, so "a" is the correct answer. When defects are detected by examination during production, rework and additional testing is required. The process loses efficiency and the opportunity for profit is diminished. Another result of internal failure cost is excessive product scrap buildup. That requires additional handling and disposition. The other three chief categories of failure cost are: appraisal costs, prevention costs, and external failure costs.

50. B: External failures costs are those expenses resulting from product defects that appear after the customer has purchased the product, so answer "b" is correct. It is an external failure cost when product defects reach the customer and result in expensive warranty and return transactions. The money spent on preventing and detecting product or service defects throughout the production process, from design until final sales and beyond, can be divided into four categories: internal failures, external failures, appraisal costs, and prevention costs.

How to Overcome Test Anxiety

Just the thought of taking a test is enough to make most people a little nervous. A test is an important event that can have a long-term impact on your future, so it's important to take it seriously and it's natural to feel anxious about performing well. But just because anxiety is normal, that doesn't mean that it's helpful in test taking, or that you should simply accept it as part of your life. Anxiety can have a variety of effects. These effects can be mild, like making you feel slightly nervous, or severe, like blocking your ability to focus or remember even a simple detail.

If you experience test anxiety—whether severe or mild—it's important to know how to beat it. To discover this, first you need to understand what causes test anxiety.

Causes of Test Anxiety

While we often think of anxiety as an uncontrollable emotional state, it can actually be caused by simple, practical things. One of the most common causes of test anxiety is that a person does not feel adequately prepared for their test. This feeling can be the result of many different issues such as poor study habits or lack of organization, but the most common culprit is time management. Starting to study too late, failing to organize your study time to cover all of the material, or being distracted while you study will mean that you're not well prepared for the test. This may lead to cramming the night before, which will cause you to be physically and mentally exhausted for the test. Poor time management also contributes to feelings of stress, fear, and hopelessness as you realize you are not well prepared but don't know what to do about it.

Other times, test anxiety is not related to your preparation for the test but comes from unresolved fear. This may be a past failure on a test, or poor performance on tests in general. It may come from comparing yourself to others who seem to be performing better or from the stress of living up to expectations. Anxiety may be driven by fears of the future—how failure on this test would affect your educational and career goals. These fears are often completely irrational, but they can still negatively impact your test performance.

Elements of Test Anxiety

As mentioned earlier, test anxiety is considered to be an emotional state, but it has physical and mental components as well. Sometimes you may not even realize that you are suffering from test anxiety until you notice the physical symptoms. These can include trembling hands, rapid heartbeat, sweating, nausea, and tense muscles. Extreme anxiety may lead to fainting or vomiting. Obviously, any of these symptoms can have a negative impact on testing. It is important to recognize them as soon as they begin to occur so that you can address the problem before it damages your performance.

The mental components of test anxiety include trouble focusing and inability to remember learned information. During a test, your mind is on high alert, which can help you recall information and stay focused for an extended period of time. However, anxiety interferes with your mind's natural processes, causing you to blank out, even on the questions you know well. The strain of testing during anxiety makes it difficult to stay focused, especially on a test that may take several hours. Extreme anxiety can take a huge mental toll, making it difficult not only to recall test information but even to understand the test questions or pull your thoughts together.

Effects of Test Anxiety

Test anxiety is like a disease—if left untreated, it will get progressively worse. Anxiety leads to poor performance, and this reinforces the feelings of fear and failure, which in turn lead to poor performances on subsequent tests. It can grow from a mild nervousness to a crippling condition. If allowed to progress, test anxiety can have a big impact on your schooling, and consequently on your future.

Test anxiety can spread to other parts of your life. Anxiety on tests can become anxiety in any stressful situation, and blanking on a test can turn into panicking in a job situation. But fortunately, you don't have to let anxiety rule your testing and determine your grades. There are a number of relatively simple steps you can take to move past anxiety and function normally on a test and in the rest of life.

Physical Steps for Beating Test Anxiety

While test anxiety is a serious problem, the good news is that it can be overcome. It doesn't have to control your ability to think and remember information. While it may take time, you can begin taking steps today to beat anxiety.

Just as your first hint that you may be struggling with anxiety comes from the physical symptoms, the first step to treating it is also physical. Rest is crucial for having a clear, strong mind. If you are tired, it is much easier to give in to anxiety. But if you establish good sleep habits, your body and mind will be ready to perform optimally, without the strain of exhaustion. Additionally, sleeping well helps you to retain information better, so you're more likely to recall the answers when you see the test questions.

Getting good sleep means more than going to bed on time. It's important to allow your brain time to relax. Take study breaks from time to time so it doesn't get overworked, and don't study right before bed. Take time to rest your mind before trying to rest your body, or you may find it difficult to fall asleep.

Along with sleep, other aspects of physical health are important in preparing for a test. Good nutrition is vital for good brain function. Sugary foods and drinks may give a burst of energy but this burst is followed by a crash, both physically and emotionally. Instead, fuel your body with protein and vitamin-rich foods.

Also, drink plenty of water. Dehydration can lead to headaches and exhaustion, especially if your brain is already under stress from the rigors of the test. Particularly if your test is a long one, drink water during the breaks. And if possible, take an energy-boosting snack to eat between sections.

Along with sleep and diet, a third important part of physical health is exercise. Maintaining a steady workout schedule is helpful, but even taking 5-minute study breaks to walk can help get your blood pumping faster and clear your head. Exercise also releases endorphins, which contribute to a positive feeling and can help combat test anxiety.

When you nurture your physical health, you are also contributing to your mental health. If your body is healthy, your mind is much more likely to be healthy as well. So take time to rest, nourish your body with healthy food and water, and get moving as much as possible. Taking these physical steps will make you stronger and more able to take the mental steps necessary to overcome test anxiety.

Mental Steps for Beating Test Anxiety

Working on the mental side of test anxiety can be more challenging, but as with the physical side, there are clear steps you can take to overcome it. As mentioned earlier, test anxiety often stems from lack of preparation, so the obvious solution is to prepare for the test. Effective studying may be the most important weapon you have for beating test anxiety, but you can and should employ several other mental tools to combat fear.

First, boost your confidence by reminding yourself of past success—tests or projects that you aced. If you're putting as much effort into preparing for this test as you did for those, there's no reason you should expect to fail here. Work hard to prepare; then trust your preparation.

Second, surround yourself with encouraging people. It can be helpful to find a study group, but be sure that the people you're around will encourage a positive attitude. If you spend time with others who are anxious or cynical, this will only contribute to your own anxiety. Look for others who are motivated to study hard from a desire to succeed, not from a fear of failure.

Third, reward yourself. A test is physically and mentally tiring, even without anxiety, and it can be helpful to have something to look forward to. Plan an activity following the test, regardless of the outcome, such as going to a movie or getting ice cream.

When you are taking the test, if you find yourself beginning to feel anxious, remind yourself that you know the material. Visualize successfully completing the test. Then take a few deep, relaxing breaths and return to it. Work through the questions carefully but with confidence, knowing that you are capable of succeeding.

Developing a healthy mental approach to test taking will also aid in other areas of life. Test anxiety affects more than just the actual test—it can be damaging to your mental health and even contribute to depression. It's important to beat test anxiety before it becomes a problem for more than testing.

Study Strategy

Being prepared for the test is necessary to combat anxiety, but what does being prepared look like? You may study for hours on end and still not feel prepared. What you need is a strategy for test prep. The next few pages outline our recommended steps to help you plan out and conquer the challenge of preparation.

Step 1: Scope Out the Test

Learn everything you can about the format (multiple choice, essay, etc.) and what will be on the test. Gather any study materials, course outlines, or sample exams that may be available. Not only will this help you to prepare, but knowing what to expect can help to alleviate test anxiety.

Step 2: Map Out the Material

Look through the textbook or study guide and make note of how many chapters or sections it has. Then divide these over the time you have. For example, if a book has 15 chapters and you have five days to study, you need to cover three chapters each day. Even better, if you have the time, leave an extra day at the end for overall review after you have gone through the material in depth.

If time is limited, you may need to prioritize the material. Look through it and make note of which sections you think you already have a good grasp on, and which need review. While you are studying, skim quickly through the familiar sections and take more time on the challenging parts.

Write out your plan so you don't get lost as you go. Having a written plan also helps you feel more in control of the study, so anxiety is less likely to arise from feeling overwhelmed at the amount to cover.

Step 3: Gather Your Tools

Decide what study method works best for you. Do you prefer to highlight in the book as you study and then go back over the highlighted portions? Or do you type out notes of the important information? Or is it helpful to make flashcards that you can carry with you? Assemble the pens, index cards, highlighters, post-it notes, and any other materials you may need so you won't be distracted by getting up to find things while you study.

If you're having a hard time retaining the information or organizing your notes, experiment with different methods. For example, try color-coding by subject with colored pens, highlighters, or post-it notes. If you learn better by hearing, try recording yourself reading your notes so you can listen while in the car, working out, or simply sitting at your desk. Ask a friend to quiz you from your flashcards, or try teaching someone the material to solidify it in your mind.

Step 4: Create Your Environment

It's important to avoid distractions while you study. This includes both the obvious distractions like visitors and the subtle distractions like an uncomfortable chair (or a too-comfortable couch that makes you want to fall asleep). Set up the best study environment possible: good lighting and a comfortable work area. If background music helps you focus, you may want to turn it on, but otherwise keep the room quiet. If you are using a computer to take notes, be sure you don't have any other windows open, especially applications like social media, games, or anything else that could distract you. Silence your phone and turn off notifications. Be sure to keep water close by so you stay hydrated while you study (but avoid unhealthy drinks and snacks).

Also, take into account the best time of day to study. Are you freshest first thing in the morning? Try to set aside some time then to work through the material. Is your mind clearer in the afternoon or evening? Schedule your study session then. Another method is to study at the same time of day that you will take the test, so that your brain gets used to working on the material at that time and will be ready to focus at test time.

Step 5: Study!

Once you have done all the study preparation, it's time to settle into the actual studying. Sit down, take a few moments to settle your mind so you can focus, and begin to follow your study plan. Don't give in to distractions or let yourself procrastinate. This is your time to prepare so you'll be ready to fearlessly approach the test. Make the most of the time and stay focused.

Of course, you don't want to burn out. If you study too long you may find that you're not retaining the information very well. Take regular study breaks. For example, taking five minutes out of every hour to walk briskly, breathing deeply and swinging your arms, can help your mind stay fresh.

As you get to the end of each chapter or section, it's a good idea to do a quick review. Remind yourself of what you learned and work on any difficult parts. When you feel that you've mastered the material, move on to the next part. At the end of your study session, briefly skim through your notes again.

But while review is helpful, cramming last minute is NOT. If at all possible, work ahead so that you won't need to fit all your study into the last day. Cramming overloads your brain with more information than it can process and retain, and your tired mind may struggle to recall even previously learned information when it is overwhelmed with last-minute study. Also, the urgent nature of cramming and the stress placed on your brain contribute to anxiety. You'll be more likely to go to the test feeling unprepared and having trouble thinking clearly.

So don't cram, and don't stay up late before the test, even just to review your notes at a leisurely pace. Your brain needs rest more than it needs to go over the information again. In fact, plan to finish your studies by noon or early afternoon the day before the test. Give your brain the rest of the day to relax or focus on other things, and get a good night's sleep. Then you will be fresh for the test and better able to recall what you've studied.

Step 6: Take a Practice Test

Many courses offer sample tests, either online or in the study materials. This is an excellent resource to check whether you have mastered the material, as well as to prepare for the test format and environment.

Check the test format ahead of time: the number of questions, the type (multiple choice, free response, etc.), and the time limit. Then create a plan for working through them. For example, if you have 30 minutes to take a 60-question test, your limit is 30 seconds per question. Spend less time on the questions you know well so that you can take more time on the difficult ones.

If you have time to take several practice tests, take the first one open book, with no time limit. Work through the questions at your own pace and make sure you fully understand them. Gradually work up to taking a test under test conditions: sit at a desk with all study materials put away and set a timer. Pace yourself to make sure you finish the test with time to spare and go back to check your answers if you have time.

After each test, check your answers. On the questions you missed, be sure you understand why you missed them. Did you misread the question (tests can use tricky wording)? Did you forget the information? Or was it something you hadn't learned? Go back and study any shaky areas that the practice tests reveal.

Taking these tests not only helps with your grade, but also aids in combating test anxiety. If you're already used to the test conditions, you're less likely to worry about it, and working through tests until you're scoring well gives you a confidence boost. Go through the practice tests until you feel comfortable, and then you can go into the test knowing that you're ready for it.

Test Tips

On test day, you should be confident, knowing that you've prepared well and are ready to answer the questions. But aside from preparation, there are several test day strategies you can employ to maximize your performance.

First, as stated before, get a good night's sleep the night before the test (and for several nights before that, if possible). Go into the test with a fresh, alert mind rather than staying up late to study.

Try not to change too much about your normal routine on the day of the test. It's important to eat a nutritious breakfast, but if you normally don't eat breakfast at all, consider eating just a protein bar. If you're a coffee drinker, go ahead and have your normal coffee. Just make sure you time it so that the caffeine doesn't wear off right in the middle of your test. Avoid sugary beverages, and drink enough water to stay hydrated but not so much that you need a restroom break 10 minutes into the test. If your test isn't first thing in the morning, consider going for a walk or doing a light workout before the test to get your blood flowing.

Allow yourself enough time to get ready, and leave for the test with plenty of time to spare so you won't have the anxiety of scrambling to arrive in time. Another reason to be early is to select a good seat. It's helpful to sit away from doors and windows, which can be distracting. Find a good seat, get out your supplies, and settle your mind before the test begins.

When the test begins, start by going over the instructions carefully, even if you already know what to expect. Make sure you avoid any careless mistakes by following the directions.

Then begin working through the questions, pacing yourself as you've practiced. If you're not sure on an answer, don't spend too much time on it, and don't let it shake your confidence. Either skip it and come back later, or eliminate as many wrong answers as possible and guess among the remaining ones. Don't dwell on these questions as you continue—put them out of your mind and focus on what lies ahead.

Be sure to read all of the answer choices, even if you're sure the first one is the right answer. Sometimes you'll find a better one if you keep reading. But don't second-guess yourself if you do immediately know the answer. Your gut instinct is usually right. Don't let test anxiety rob you of the information you know.

If you have time at the end of the test (and if the test format allows), go back and review your answers. Be cautious about changing any, since your first instinct tends to be correct, but make sure you didn't misread any of the questions or accidentally mark the wrong answer choice. Look over any you skipped and make an educated guess.

At the end, leave the test feeling confident. You've done your best, so don't waste time worrying about your performance or wishing you could change anything. Instead, celebrate the successful completion of this test. And finally, use this test to learn how to deal with anxiety even better next time.

Review Video: Test Anxiety
Visit mometrix.com/academy and enter code: 100340

Important Qualification

Not all anxiety is created equal. If your test anxiety is causing major issues in your life beyond the classroom or testing center, or if you are experiencing troubling physical symptoms related to your anxiety, it may be a sign of a serious physiological or psychological condition. If this sounds like your situation, we strongly encourage you to seek professional help.

Online Resources

Due to our efforts to try to keep this book to a manageable length, we've created a link that will give you access to all of your online resources:

mometrix.com/resources719/cpimsmr

It's Your Moment, Let's Celebrate It!

Share your story @mometrixtestpreparation